THE FOREST

OTHER TITLES BY ROGER A. CARAS

AVAILABLE IN BISON BOOK EDITIONS

The Custer Wolf:
Biography of an American Renegade

Monarch of Deadman Bay:
The Life and Death of a Kodiak Bear

Panther!

Source of the Thunder:
The Biography of a California Condor

ROGER CARAS
THE FOREST

Illustrations by Norman Arlott

UNIVERSITY OF NEBRASKA PRESS

LINCOLN

First Bison Book printing: 1991
Most recent printing indicated by the last digit below:
10   9   8   7   6   5   4   3   2   1

Library of Congress Cataloging-in-Publication Data
Caras, Roger A.
The forest / Roger Caras: illustrations by Norman Arlott.
p.   cm.
Reprint. Originally published: New York: Holt, Rinehart and Winston, c1979.
ISBN 0-8032-6342-2 (pbk.)
1. Forest ecology—Northwestern States.   2. Forest ecology—Northwest, Pacific.
I. Title.
[QH104.5.N62C37   1991]
574.5'2642'09795—dc20
90-49910   CIP

Reprinted by arrangement with Roger A. Caras

FOR JILL, PAMELA, CLAY
. . . AND STEVE

Acknowledgments

Even when an author appears to work alone he is engaged in a kind of team effort. To Helene Curtis, who read the manuscript in its first draft and sharpened language and intercepted inherent vice, I am grateful. To my loyal and able assistant, Don Wall, who labored in many different ways, my thanks for helping to make it a better book. Norman Arlott's drawings add a new and important dimension and were a much appreciated labor of love. Don Hutter's input went far beyond that of an editor. He helped make it a much truer picture of the forest by day and by night.

Douglas fir cone

western hemlock cone

THE FOREST

1

On a dozen levels, each discrete and assertive, the air moved across the land. Undulating like sheets on a restless sea, the eddying winds moved from somewhere to everywhere, their unseen shape repeating the shape of the land. Where the land rose, the layers of restless energy rose, and where ancient rivers and thrusting earth had cracked and cut deep valleys in the surface, the avenues of air dipped, too. It was of the history of the land, then, that the air now spoke in soft whistles, murmurs, and hums.

There were other forces that shaped these high lanes in the sky. Heated air, energized by sun careening off rocks and canyon walls, lost its weight and rose. Often these jets and spirals gained velocity from the cut of the canyon itself and spurted high, lifting the cooler airstreams into which they sliced. Coming up from below, they struck like dull knives into rubber sheets. The effect of all this was a tricky and turbulent sky, the kind in which eagles like to play.

Aquila chrysaëtos, the golden eagle, came in over a high ledge in the east and felt the turbulence beneath her. She sailed on wings nearly eight feet across. She was almost black underneath, evenly so except for some white at the base of her tail. But the gold above, especially on her neck, glistened and marked her as one of her kind. An inexperienced eye could mistake her for an immature bald eagle, but she was larger than the bald, with which she often shared her sky, and darker, too. And whereas the bald eagle had bare feet, the golden's were feathered to the toes.

Shortly before she soared in over the eastern ridge, the eagle had fed. She had spotted a rabbit from 6,000 feet and had dropped, swooping in so as to approach from behind. The rabbit, as keenly equipped to flee as the eagle was to attack, had spotted her and started away in a frantic, jagged course. The chase had had the same meaning for each participant, survival. The rushing dive of the eagle was swifter than the mad dash of the rabbit, however, and 75 feet from where it had started for distant cover the small mammal was picked off the ground and dropped back again.

It had died on contact, though, for the eagle's talons had rolled shut and snapped the spine of her prey. Because rabbits usually lose and eagles win, there are millions of rabbits born each year, far more than the number of hunting birds. Still, it is the victim that controls the population of the predator. The number of eagles depends on the supply of their food base—rabbits and other prey—and not the other way around.

Because of her extreme agility and the athletic rate at which she lives, the eagle has rapid metabolism. She needs food often and quickly. As she came in across the ridge, she was already using up the substance she had borrowed from the land in the form of the rabbit. Soon it would be time to hunt again.

In a creature that must use the sky to survive, body weight and its distribution are critical factors of life. In small birds the weight of leg musculature is slight, for the legs play a minor role in survival. In an eagle, whose legs are killing machines and which must be able to run to take off after a heavy meal, the leg muscles are powerful and heavy. The weight of the flight muscles, too, is critical. In the coot, an indifferent flier at best, barely more than 10 percent of the bird's total weight is assigned to the muscles of flight; in the golden eagle it is at least 25 percent. The bewildering aerial maneuvers of eagle flight are made possible by this critical distribution of weight—the heavy working muscles richly supplied with food; light, hollow bones; and the segmented structure and versatility of the wings. Each feather is a complex machine of its own, and the relationship of one feather to another is an equally complex, interlocking mechanical process. The deeply notched feather structure at the trailing edge of the wing provides that wing with many wings of its own, for that is what each feather becomes. A split-wing cascade effect is created by each feather's being stepped behind and above the one before. These structures are continuously variable and movable, and the result is an animal able to play with the wind, to make a game of the sky.

An eagle on the ground is a large and rather clumsy bird. It can become airborne only after taxiing. *Aquila*, after feeding on the rabbit, had used 50 feet of runway, leaving behind talon imprints of her strides, before there was enough air under her wings and enough velocity for the driving downthrusts to lift her away. But now that she was well free of the earth, she was truly the eagle, her flight expressible as poetry or as mathematical formulas. An engineer might define her wing as $F(m_2)$ and speak of her lift force as $H = C_a F v^2 p/2$. Poets, seeing the same miracle above their heads, might sing of God and wind and golden sun playing on golden bird. It was *Aquila*, the eagle of gold, that slipped through layer after layer of blanketing air in search of a place to rest in the valley below and that finally picked the jutting branch of a hemlock standing straight out from its tall trunk.

She had seen her tree and picked her branch at 4,000 feet. Her eyes, a thousand times more keen than our own, scanned the trees and the open areas between them. A powerful bird when obtaining and protecting her food, she still avoided trouble; she lived alone and preferred having no interference where she roosted. As she swung down toward the canyon where the tree she had selected grew, her eyes picked out another object almost 10 miles away. It was a small dark spot soaring past a high pile of powder-puff clouds in an otherwise unmarred blue sky. She knew at once it was the bald eagle, *Haliaeetus leucocephalus*. With the slightest adjustments of shoulder angle and biting edges of wing, she checked her rate of descent, leveled off, then began to climb. The wind rushed beneath her and buoyed her up. The bald eagle, when he passed, would be below her. She leveled at 5,000 feet, turned her body on its own axis, shifted her long tail feathers, and curved around in a circle 4 miles across.

The bald eagle had also seen the golden hen. He did not fear her, although experience had taught him she would not let him pass without some gesture, some ritual of sky encounter. He soared on barely moving wings, for he had the wind with him at his level. Small thermals rising beneath him tilted one wing, then the other, but fine adjustments compensated easily, and his course remained unchanged.

When they were about a mile apart, the golden hen rolled off her layer of wind and dropped on her left wing. Accelerating to more than 80 miles per hour, she plummeted toward an intersecting course with the bald eagle male and, when only 30 yards separated them, rolled over on her back. Righting herself slightly, she corrected her trajectory, then rolled over on her back again and shot underneath the smaller bird upside down at 50 miles per hour.

A collision at that speed would have destroyed both birds, but *Aquila* only brushed the bald eagle, grabbing away a few feathers in her talons as they passed. Fifty yards beyond him, she let the feathers go and spiraled

5

down after them. They were lost in the trees by the time she thrust her feet out in front of her, dropped her tail, and braked to land on the branch she had selected ten minutes earlier. From her first sighting of the bald eagle, through her climb to 5,000 feet above the valley floor, through her plunging dive and roll and her brushing of the other bird, then her descent to the branch, it had all been liquid geometry in the sky. She had done it, perhaps, as a signal that the sky above the

Aquila only brushed the bald eagle, grabbing away a few feathers—

valley was hers, that the bald eagle was passing through her territory. Or perhaps it was done just because the golden eagle felt like asserting herself—her strength and her skill. By the time her talons closed on wood the bald eagle was gone, over the ridge in the east to seek a lake in another valley where he could fish and look for carrion. The golden eagle rolled forward slightly on her feet, lifted her tail, and splattered her excrement onto the forest floor. Some of the rabbit's

substance was returned to earth. The planet would have to wait for the rest until the eagle herself died.

In the science of botany there are plants known as the umbelliferous ones, the bearers of umbels. In each of these there is an inflorescence of small flower stalks, very often equal in length, which rise up from a common center. Many of our familiar plants belong to this type; carrots, celery, parsnip, and parsley are among them. Hemlock, an herb, is such a plant. It has been one of the most infamous plant names in all history, for it is said to have taken the life of Socrates. There can be little doubt that in several classical periods of the ancient world this waterside herb was used to manipulate the succession of thrones and royal families. Hemlock, the killer of kings, however, is not related to the hemlock in which the eagle settled. It is only an herb and nothing like a giant tree.

The hemlock tree, *Tsuga*, is one of a small group of trees found in America and Asia and nowhere else. It is related to the spruces and in appearance reminds one of those cousin trees and perhaps of the yews. An elegant tree seen in the overall, it stands as a giant seemingly at peace with itself and with the surrounding Douglas firs with which it is almost always associated.

The greatest of all the hemlock trees is the western one, *Tsuga heterophylla*, the kind in which the eagle sat. Standing 6,000 feet above sea level, it is one of the largest, most brilliantly green, most majestic and serene of trees. It grows where it will seldom be stressed by want of water. It thrives in periods of constant mist, in

places of ferns and deep vegetable litter. It is little won-
der that an endless parade of life comes to the hemlock
to live and die and convolute itself around and through
the endless exchange of chemicals that permeate and
surround the tree. The hemlock provides a sensuous
matrix, and whereas its namesake in Europe was
known as the taker of life, the philosopher's and
prince's bane, the American tree is the giver of life and
thereby has a softer place in both natural history and
the historic affairs of man.

2

 The hemlock on which the eagle had landed was more than 450 years old and stood 200 feet tall. Its kind came into being before even the dinosaurs walked the earth—needle bearers to fill the first dryland forests—millions of years before the oaks and elms, the walnuts and aspens, and other more complex trees came into being. Grass came later, too, and so did wild flowers and all flowering plants.

The last glacial period, between ten and twelve thousand years ago, was unkind to the hemlocks of North America. They existed through that period, true enough, and survived, but in smaller numbers, in fewer places, and perhaps in smaller sizes. About nine thousand years ago, in a kinder era known as the Pre-Boreal, things were better suited to the hemlock kind. By the time the Boreal period of 6000 B.C. was upon

The golden eagle rolled forward slightly on her feet.

their land the hemlocks were in command of their part of the woodlands. And although the signs are small and slow in revealing themselves, the weather has cooled since then, since about 4000 B.C., and it is possible that the hemlock hold has slipped accordingly. Such changes are not directly visible to an unaided eye with a limited span of years, and only the count of seed and pollen left unrealized in soil deposits can prove or disprove such theories. But the hemlock still flourishes and enriches a world that must in turn be rich for the tree to thrive.

Hemlocks are simple trees. The cones that protect the seeds and the needles that are their true leaves are of a primitive but highly successful design. The cones exist for the single purpose of holding the seeds of the future until it is time for them to be dispersed. They are tough, those cones, with each scale harboring two unshielded 1/8-inch-long seeds at its base. There is no anther, no stigma, no ovary—all refined parts belonging to younger species. The hemlock needle is dark green, shiny, and grooved above. Straight and plain, it is protected against weather changes by a coating of wax. Resin helps hold off the effects of decay. The roots of the tree run deep and are more simply designed than those of species that came later. The hemlock is an ultimate tree, a tree unadorned by climbers or runners or bushy growth.

From Alaska to California, discontinuously, the flexibly tipped western hemlock shares the great upland forests with the Douglas fir, the Sitka spruce (lower down), western red cedar, alpine fir, red fir and white.

Massive and bothered by few insects, these conifers preside over a complex web of animal and plant life and some forms in between. Spawns of a temperate maritime climate of great stability, the trees stand for centuries, in some species for millennia. As they reach great age, their needle weight increases, and the massive branches interlock, sealing off the forest floor below from the rays of the sun that have, up to then, shone through like the light shafts in a cathedral. Eventually, though, the mass of the needles becomes so great that the trees prune themselves, as branches crash down to add to the debris on the forest floor and allow smaller, younger trees their time in the sun. It is then that the western hemlock flourishes in a world of giants. Along with the silver fir and some of the cedars, it grows toward the sky.

Very often younger trees grow up from patriarchs that have been toppled by wind and rot. The ancient trees down in the evolving humus become the nurse logs upon which the future grows. That was how this tree, the hemlock on which the eagle rested, began. Almost half a millennium ago, a cone on its parent tree had matured and opened, releasing the seeds, which then fell to the ground. One seed had been blown sideways by the wind and had landed on an older giant that had died and begun to decay. Falling into a small crevice of this nurse tree, the seed had waited. Inside the seed an embryo tree lay, with all its leaves, its stem, its critical root point. Rain and sun came in proper sequence and intervals. The needs of a new generation were met.

The embryo began to grow. There was enough warmth, enough moisture and nutrients surrounding it both within and without the seedcase for its growth and survival. The growing embryo split the seed, and the tough root point emerged. It bent over and began to grow down, invading the decaying fibers of the nurse tree. Soon the tiny point was drawing both food and water from the old tree and the soil it was rapidly joining. Needle-shaped leaves pulled free from the seedcase as the tree passed its next critical test. It began manufacturing its own food. Root hairs had formed deep down where the root point led, and the terminal bud below the empty, unattached seedcase lay beside an infant tree on its way to the sky.

All things on earth are finite. All the needles in all the coniferous forests are measurable. If they seem without bounds, it is our inability to comprehend them that is at fault. Our only encounter with the unmeasurable occurs once our thoughts leave this planet. Infinity is probably a temporary condition, however. As the life-span of stars and species goes, it may one day be a classroom toy for slow learners.

Among the finite substances on and around our planet the masses of which we guess at still, rather than truly weigh, are the gases oxygen and carbon dioxide. Life on earth is wholly dependent on them. We believe now, although our scales and yardsticks are not as precise in the great affairs of our environment as we would like, that the carbon dioxide in our atmosphere is renewed once every three hundred years. Using the same primitive tools, we have come to be-

lieve that the free oxygen in our planet's system is renewed every two thousand years. These facts, whatever
their actual dimensions, tie us to the tree and the tree to
the eagle. We all are locked into a web of exchange.

An estimate generally accepted today places the
amount of carbon dioxide processed annually on earth
at 200 billion tons. Of that conversion, probably 80 percent occurs in the upper layers of the ocean where an
unimaginable, if entirely measurable, number of minute plants live. The other 20 percent, still a critically
high percentage, apparently occurs in the gardens of
the world, both the gardens of man and the gardens of
nature, such as the forest in which the eagle sat.

This processing of carbon dioxide, known as photosynthesis, was operating within the infant western
hemlock from its first exposure to the sun. Light falling
on its needles and leaves was absorbed as energy. Free
energy, always available in every daylit hour, fed the
forest through each of the green plants growing there.
The work was done in each by a pigment in the leaves
called chlorophyll. That was the principal pigment at
least, but there were, in fact, others working at other
places in the spectrum.

In a miraculous link to the cosmos, light supplied the
energy required by each plant to produce the organic
molecules which compose all living things. Each green
plant, green because of chlorophyll, was able to extract
the free carbon dioxide surrounding it in the air and
cause it to react with water from the air and soil and
form organic compounds. It stored chemical energy for
growing cells. As this occurred, oxygen was released

into the atmosphere as a kind of exhaust fume. Animal life in great part sustains its cells with the waste products of plants. If the hemlock could have absorbed light of only one wavelength, however, a large part of the sunlight that plowed into the forest's depths from distant space would have been irretrievably lost. Although chlorophyll could work alone, could transfer carbon dioxide and water and light into the hard substances of life, photosynthesis is most efficient when two or more pigments work together. Light in shorter wavelengths falling on the hemlocks, lost on chlorophyll, was trapped by its companion pigments. When the reddish beta-carotene rejected the red or long wavelengths— that is, left them for chlorophyll to deal with—almost the entire visible spectrum was put to use by the tree.

The state of energy conversion was stable, long-lived, and uninterrupted and would remain that way as long as that energy was available to the forest. While photosynthesis was proceeding rapidly in one cell of the hemlock, that cell had the ability to store light energy or pass it along to neighboring chlorophyll molecules for immediate or future use. The sun's energy was shunted from cell to cell within each needle on the tree, and energy that might have been lost as heat became the stuff of photosynthesis where and when it was needed.

The needle-shaped leaves of the hemlock no less than the eagle were bathed by energy born in the nuclear holocaust we call the sun. That sun, although 93 million miles away from the forest (that is, 270 times closer than

Proxima Centauri, the next nearest star), was as much a part of the forest and the life cycle of the eagle and the hemlock as any object or force close enough for either to touch. The eagle and the tree were of Earth, and Earth is of a system tied to Sol, our sun, and Sol contains 99.9 percent of all the mass of our entire system.

The continuous nuclear explosion that is a star came to earth and visited the eagle and the hemlock with energy made benevolent by the length of its journey. Their kinds were born of that energy and forever linked to it. The human co-planeteers of the eagle and the tree can never forget that their subjects are, like themselves, linked to a cosmos. That is the larger truth of the tree and the eagle, their link with everything that has ever been, everything that is, and everything that can ever be. It is in this concept that so many people see a master plan. If the plan does in fact exist, the assault by some upon the tree, upon the bird, and upon man, who alone on earth can think of these things, is most difficult to comprehend. He who would strike the bird or the tree or man strikes at a child of the sun, and the anger of that parent is beyond the farthest edge of the human mind.

The tree was a perfect combination of elements, each of them reflecting the years of the giant's growing. In the center lay the heartwood. It was the supporting column of the mature tree. Heartwood is dead, it cannot grow, but it will not decay or fail the tree by losing strength as long as the rest of the tree remains intact and in balance with its surroundings. Girding the central column was the sapwood. Through it ran the pipelines that carried water from the roots to the leaves. As the inner layers of sapwood lose their vitality, they join the center column as heartwood. Surrounding the sapwood was a thin but vital layer known as the cambium. Each year, stimulated by auxins, or hormones, this layer produces both new bark and new sapwood on its outer and inner surfaces. Lying outside the cambium layer was the part of the tree known as the phloem. Just as the sapwood carried water from the roots up to the leaves, the phloem carried food down from the leaves to the rest of the tree. As growth continued within the cambium layer, the phloem was pushed out to become true bark. And beyond the phloem was that bark, the means by which the tree protected itself against heat and cold and some enemies.

These transitions, sapwood to heartwood, cambium layer to sapwood and phloem, and phloem to bark will continue as long as the tree is alive. When they stop, the tree will die. Its heartwood will fail soon after that, and all the chemicals the tree contains will circulate again as the tree becomes the victim of weather, fire, insects, and time. It is the chemical harmony of the forest, and if anything approaches perfection on this planet, it is that.

Even as the eagle rested, looking out across the valley floor, a war was being waged within and on the tree itself. Tree-killing bark beetles of the family Scolytidae had invaded the forest some weeks before. Working first on fallen logs, then attacking standing timber as their numbers increased, they ground and crunched their way toward the living heart of the forest. Small, dark, compact, these insects had found the tree of the eagle's perch several days earlier.

They were still trying to make inroads. The bark of the western hemlock is between an inch and an inch and a half thick. It is deeply seamed and has broad, flat ridges with close, thin cinnamon-brown scales. It was through that bark the tree killers had to bore to find the pale yellowish sapwood beneath. There, where bark and wood met, the bark beetle could excavate its tunnels and galleries and plant its eggs, from which tree-eating larvae would hatch to further the march of destruction.

When the first beetles reached the wood of the eagle's hemlock, they found a tree in water balance; within its tissues there was enough moisture, but not too much. As they began scoring the cells of the wood itself, they encountered richly laden resin cells, which exploded and killed many of the beetles before real harm could be done. Had the tree been badly stressed by drought, as can sometimes happen on western slopes, the resin would not have jetted out, and the insects could have continued their assault unimpeded. It could have meant the death of a tree. In trees like the hemlock a water shortage is felt in many ways.

The hemlock had outside allies in its war against the invading tree killers. The Cleridae, checkered beetles, voracious predators faster than the bark borers, had swarmed into the area when the bark beetles first began settling in. The female bark beetles had sent out chemical messages, pheromones intended to attract males from miles around, but the checkered hunters had detected them, too, and responded on a different kind of errand. They pounced upon all the exposed bark beetles they could find and devoured them. Then, where they could find holes in the bark, either they pursued the borers into their lairs and ate them there, or they deposited their eggs. Soon after those eggs hatched, the predatory larvae would follow the tunnels of the boring beetle until they came to their larvae. They would feed upon them, larvae upon larvae, related as predator and prey just like the adult forms of the two species.

Delicate brownish black braconid wasps also joined the battle. By means not really understood, these wasps follow the bark beetle infestations from forest to forest and move in at just the right time. Using complex infrared receptors to detect heat, they locate the larvae of the bark beetle behind the inch or more of thick, pulpy bark screen shielding them and drill through with their ovipositors. Thrusting their muscular abdomens downward, the wasps inject their eggs into the bodies of the bark beetle larvae. The eggs hatch there, and the emerging wasp larvae feed on their hosts. The bark beetles, once they have been injected with wasp eggs, are doomed. No force on earth can save them.

Met, then, by exploding resin cells not made flaccid by drought, attacked by hunting clerid beetles, injected with hosts of braconid wasp eggs, the invasion of bark beetles was slowing. It was a momentary setback, though, for these beetles, like all primitive life-forms, are tenacious. The bark beetle has both time and numbers on its side. One day, in this forest as in all others, harm would be done, and trees would fall, victims of small dark insects, any one of which weighs no more than a needle or two from the hemlock's smallest, farthest arms.

3

As the sun warmed the air between the trees and spiraled it upward, white pine butterflies of the family Pieridae moved along the shafts. Living dust of the forest, splendid spots of light, they ascended the spirals and drafts around the hemlock. But it was a nearby Douglas fir they sought, for it is only upon that species of tree in August that these creatures can deposit their eggs. The larvae hatching from those eggs feed on the needles of the Douglas fir, then lower themselves on threads of shimmering silk and come to rest on vegetation far below, there to pupate. They moved around the hemlock as if to convince themselves that the tree was not quite right—needled well and coned, but not the mandatory Douglas fir.

The pine butterflies were but one of the myriad

members of the biotic community alive under the perching *Aquila*. Other insects, too, rose by air or silk or wood. Spiders of the family Clubionidae drifted back and forth, their invisible silken lines sustaining them in their hunt for food. Coming upon insect prey that their eight simple eyes could detect only as a vague movement of shadow and light, they clamped chelicerae into their victims and pumped poison upward through the tips. Not only did this instantly paralyze the insects, but the poison also began to liquefy their insides, turning them into a digestible soup the spider could suck free from the hull. With no moving mouthparts, the spider must liquefy its prey before it can draw upon it for another day of life. Running to more than a million to the acre, spiders form an essential control on insect life in the forest complex.

In the upper layer near where the eagle sat, the mite *Bdella oblonga* moved unseen. A small, soft-bodied bark louse, it passed slowly along trunks and needles seeking food. Although its numbers living on the giant hemlock ran into the millions, they did the tree no harm. Winged and fast when necessary, they are related to the wingless book lice that invade human habitations and damage the most precious records of man. But these bark lice sought only the dry organic matter, the molds and fungi the tree hosted by the ton. The tree was a vast garden, and these lice but a few of the millions of its harvesters.

Collembola were there as well, minute wingless insects known as springtails, of which there are more than two thousand species in North America alone.

These hemlock-loving mites moved over the bark of the tree, seeking organic food.

Froghoppers, so named because they look in fact like tiny frogs, also fed on the tree's debris, doing less than negligible harm to their host as they hopped and skipped from bark ridge to bark ridge. They are known as spittlebugs in their nymph stage since they secrete and surround themselves with a bubbly mass resembling human spittle.

All this life moved at various layers, from earth to above the eagle's high roost. Hunting wasps, spiders, ants, and other predators stalked the smaller sucking and plant-chewing species over a battlefield so vast its soldiers, at any given moment, numbered in the tens of millions, and this was only one tree, itself one of millions. The eagle looked out across the forest canopy, uninvolved, concentrating on larger scaled wars, though war essentially no different in kind from all the others.

Not all animals that live far above the ground are minute, winged, or encased in an arthropod's shell. High in the hemlock lived *Phenacomys silvicola*, the tree mouse. A small animal 4 inches long with another 3 inches of naked tail, a reddish back, and markedly gray sides, it can be found anywhere from 15 to 100 feet above the ground. Tree mice may spend their entire lives in a single tree. Their naked, blind young may be born in any month, for these mice do not hibernate. The nest, crammed in where a branch and the trunk of a tree meet, may contain half a bushel of pine needles and other plant debris. Feathers, too, and spider webs, anything that can bring strength and resist rain and wind, may be incorporated to secure the home of the helpless young. The nest is built upon year after year and grows in time into a fortress.

Adult tree mice are more cautious than many other arboreal species. They move along branches slowly and with care, testing, being certain of every step. Strangely, although their life is spent aloft, they have not gained the squirrel's speed and agility. Each step is as if on a circus wire, hesitant and uncertain and apparently truly hazardous.

On this day, almost in the shadow of the eagle hen, a male tree mouse moved out from his nest. He was seeking fresh needles on which to feed, and sensing no immediate danger, he moved along the branch away from the trunk. The eagle saw him but decided he was not enough. She looked away. But other eyes followed the mouse's progress.

On another hemlock 50 feet away, *Surnia ulula*, the day-flying hawk owl, balanced himself with his long, rounded tail and tipped forward rather more like a sparrow hawk than an owl. He watched the mouse move farther away from the trunk and his nest. When it was too late for the mouse to turn and make his clumsy way back to his sanctuary, the owl flopped off his perch. He swooped low and then up, and as the mouse hunkered down against his fate, the owl deftly lifted him off the branch with one foot and continued in an arc back to his original perch. The golden eagle barked her *kya* sound of anger at the rude intrusion but did not pursue the matter. She did turn, however, and watch the hawk owl alight. As the smaller hunter dipped his head and decapitated the mouse, the eagle eyed her fellow predator. There were signals from inside as well as this reminder from without. Soon she, too, would have to hunt again.

Within an hour the mate of the tree mouse ventured out on the limb as well. Her motive was the same—fresh needles on which to nibble. The same hawk owl, in the same way, took the female. Again the eagle watched and called her shrill *kya kya* to the forest ears. The three newborn pink mice in the massive nest would now die slowly. Insects would feed on them before they finished their brief lives. But nature allows for this; there are many tree mice born in every hemlock forest. Their endless breeding cycle keeps their population strong.

Many small insect-eating birds make their homes in coniferous forest groves. Among the most remarkable of these birds are the family Picidae, the chisel-billed wood borers we call woodpeckers. These birds have powerful feet, usually with two toes in front and two behind. They also have stiff, spiny tails that aid them as they balance on the trunk of the tree they are punishing.

Perhaps the most remarkable thing about woodpeckers is the enormous power of their pounding thrusts and their ability to tolerate such abuse in an area as sensitive as the skull. Like all higher animals, the woodpecker has the core of its central nervous system in its head, yet it uses its head in pursuit of insects, boring into wood with a force that would stun or kill other equal-sized animals. The woodpecker has evolved with the ability to take such punishment. No woodpecker has ever been known to knock itself silly while chiseling into the wood of dead, dying, or even living trees. Its skull is very heavy for its size, its blows well aimed like those of a woodchopper, not random at all.

Among the Picidae birds that came to seek dead wood in the grove where the hemlock stood were several spectacular pileated woodpeckers. Black and crow-sized, *Dryocopus pileatus* is almost 20 inches from bill tip to tail tip. Its bright red crest, its sweeping wing-beat, and its undulating flight, exposing white under-wing areas, identify the great pileated as it moves through the forest. There are signs, too, when it has passed, for its diggings in the fallen tree trunks and stumps it has investigated will be thumb-sized and oblong.

The pileated nests in coniferous trees, particularly those that are part of a mixed forest, one like that chosen by the eagle for her perch. There, in tree holes prepared by both mating birds, three to five white eggs are laid each spring. Now that the ivory-billed woodpecker is extinct, or so nearly so it amounts to the same thing, the pileated is the largest woodpecker in all North America. Despite its great size, it lives principally on carpenter ants, which it extracts with its long, sticky tongue. Deep in their burrows in rotting timber and stumps, the ants are pursued by this spectacular bird. One wonders if nature has equipped the ants to know that the thunderous drumming on their home means a woodpecker is tearing into the wood after them, cracking apart their nests and galleys and end-lessly traveled paths. It is the sound of doom for them, but probably they are unaware.

As the eagle scanned her world, the sounds of the pileated could be heard in the grove, a machine-gun rattle of chisel bill at work, also the *kik-kikkik-kik-kikkik* song of the birds themselves as they called to each other and to the sky and to nothing in particular. In some the call was quicker than in others, and in some there were strange, complex changes in pitch.

Another family of birds that helps control insect populations is the Tyrannidae, the so-called tyrant flycatchers. Although some will eat fruit and some small reptiles, most live exclusively on insects. Unlike woodpeckers, though, the flycatchers, as their name implies, do not pursue insects in grub and larval state under bark and in wood. Sitting on exposed branches, the flycatchers wait and sally forth to snatch their food on the wing. They are fast, skilled hunters, and they seldom sing except at dawn.

One species of flycatcher in the grove that day was the enigmatic one of the western states, a member of the genus *Empidonax*, commonly called Hammond's flycatcher. Even the most ardent of bird watchers must place this one on their list with a question mark beside it. *Did I, in fact, see a Hammond's, or was it the dusky*? No one ever seems to know. The call of the Hammond's, again heard only at dawn when heard at all, is a casual, perhaps even a sloppy mixture of *se-lip*, *twur*, and *tree-ip*, or is it *clip*, *whee*, and *zee*? No one seems certain of that either.

Whether or not the olivish, yellowish, grayish little enigma of the bird watcher's world even knows its own identity, it is safe to assume the flycatcher doesn't really care except at breeding time. Its constant hunting and voracious appetite do perform a service in the forest, though, as it darts between the trees and removes insects from the air as neatly as a gardener clips a bud, and that is perhaps more important than its name.

Other birds helped as well. The hermit warbler, a tiny bird with a bright yellow head and black throat, also fed on insects, although it was nowhere near as skilled on the wing as the flycatcher. And a wheezing, buzzing *dreer zeez dreer* announced that Townsend's warbler, with its black and yellow patterned head, was working with the rest to keep the insect population down. The white-throated warbler known as the myrtle came, too, and announced itself with a *check ceek cheek*.

The many birds that added their butterfly colors to the dark green of the hemlock grove were each suited to a special place in each system they encountered at different seasons of the year. Most migrated, and each was balanced to hunt in a certain place, in a certain season, at a certain time of the day. With prey species preference, they fitted together, folded easily into each other like the fingers of two hands interlocking. Yet competition between species was at a minimum, for like all the other factors of the forest, it had been sorted out long, long ago. Those that did not fit had ceased coming or, in some cases, ceased to be. And for all those that had lasted and now belonged, there were insects enough, with billions to spare.

The western hemlock, then, lived and sustained both life and death, each phenomenon but an extension of the other. The living died, and the dead sustained the living, just as the hemlock itself was born of a nurse tree that had fallen to ground. The perfect circle of the forest turned on, as it had for hundreds of millions of years.

4

 The chemistry of a forest is a complex matrix of elements, compounds, and time. Organic matter is produced so that more organic matter of different kinds may flourish. To the forest a tree is a stage, a platform, a means of holding critical chemicals in storage and of converting others. No tree lives forever, and all chemicals return to the original mash that means continuing life in the forest.

Rocks and soil weathering in the forest itself, or high enough above it to wash down into its soil, produce calcium, potassium, magnesium, and phosphorus. Nitrogen is needed as well, but nitrogen comes from other sources, from dust and rain, even lightning. Blue-green lichens are nitrogen *fixers*. They rob the air of nitrogen and work on its chemistry in subtle ways, until the raw nitrogen is fixed into new organic compounds which reach the forest floor when rain falls and filters through the minute lichen forest. The water carries the critical compound with it as it penetrates, percolating through the forest floor debris. The chemicals also reach the soil in two other ways. When a tree itself falls, it carries its lichen burden with it, and animals that eat lichens leave nitrogen-rich droppings and eventually die and decompose or are in turn eaten and become the metabolic slag of other species.

At least 150 species of lichens inhabit the fir forests where hemlocks grow. Some species produce as much as 15 pounds of nitrogen per acre every year. Every animal and plant in the forest community, whatever its size, whatever its role, must have nitrogen, and a major source for all are the lowly lichens growing along trunks and branches, minute manufacturing centers that draw their raw materials from the air itself.

Lichens are among the least dramatic and most important life-forms on earth. They are the only plants* that can grow on otherwise barren rocks and are, in fact, one of the principal means by which rocks are decayed and turned into soil. Though edible by man, lichens taste quite bitter and are unimportant as a human food source. They do have some limited economic value in short-term projects; some lichens soaked in human urine create the dyes used in all authentic Harris tweeds, and the laboratory paper known as litmus, used in tests for acidity, comes from an

---

*Many scientists today place lichens and fungi in a kingdom of their own, no longer calling them plants at all.

extract of lichens. As so-called reindeer moss and in other forms, lichens are vital to animals both large and small.

It is difficult to imagine what the world would be like had not this association come into being. Each lichen species is the combination of two other forms, a fungus and an alga. The lichen itself is neither an alga nor a fungus, but rather both constituents locked together in an inseparable relationship.

Fungi, those relatively low forms of life that include the mushrooms, can either live free or combine in such obligate relationships with algae. For more than 350 million years, fungi have lived in a myriad of relationships, and one of the strangest is the form we call the lichen, the nitrogen fixer.

The fungus partner in most lichen species (but not all) determines the size the lichen will take and forms the bulk of the associated structure. Mycelium, for instance, is fungus material in the form of elongated tubular cells designed to invade and break down rock, wood, and bark and turn the substrate into food. The rate at which some such fungus species produce these cells is astounding. These irresistible penetrating seekers of food may grow as rapidly as 1/8,000 of an inch per minute. Each cell of the mycelium consists of a wall of chitin—not unlike the exoskeleton of insects—that contains the living material of the plant itself: the protoplasm and one or more nuclei to signal and control the unit. It is the whole of the forest reduced to microscopic size, the endless repetition getting smaller and smaller until it drops below the range of human vision.

Once a fungus member of lichen relationship has colonized the bark of a large tree, its hyphal tubes begin their spreading invasion. Soon a network has formed within which semigelatin motes of algae are enmeshed. The fungi network and the algae prisoners together constitute what we call lichen. That is the association arrived at so many millions of years ago, which allows many lichens to fix nitrogen and give it up to leaching rain and dew to feed the soil in which the hemlock grows. These life-forms use the tree as a platform and feed in part from its bark. The bark, in turn, feeds the roots of that host tree and all other life in the forest. Thus hemlock and fungi draw on common sources and serve common ends. It is, again, the chemical web of life, the utter perfection of the natural order.

The partner known as algae can in some lichen species be the dominant form, but in most cases it is not. The algae held in bondage by the fungus on the hemlock where the eagle sat were tamed almost as if they were being cultivated as a slave plant. In nearby ponds and streams grew algae very similar in structure to those forms in the lichen combinations, but not quite the same. While these stream and pond forms can live free and apart from all associations, the forms on the hemlock are as dependent on their fungus hosts as their hosts are on them. They are the Siamese twins of the plant or near-plant world, their union defying the skill of any surgeon's knife. Evolution joined them, and only that same force can separate them, although that does not seem likely to happen.

Even as the lichen spreads from branch to branch and

from tree to tree, it is done as a combined effort. The fruiting bodies which fungi normally use to reproduce are largely useless when they come from a lichen union. The lichen reproduces by an action again combined. Tiny clumps form as a few algal cells are entangled in strands of fungal mycelium. The whole carpet of lichen becomes littered by these clumps, and the wind vectors them from place to place. Thus the partners of the lichen association reproduce without benefit of a sexual relationship.

They land and begin to establish new carpets on which new populations of insects will feed, to be fed on, in turn, by other insects and arachnids, this while nitrogen is being drawn from the air and carried to the soil. The relationships of these elements remain largely mysteries—as each new apparent rule is recognized, new exceptions seem to appear. Yet we can say that this incredible complexity of life on a single standing tree is a universe in miniature. And over all, like a god of that cosmos, the eagle perched and waited until hunger or the urge to play with the wind would launch her free to enter again into a system of her own.

5

Rising from the thick broth of an early sea, the hemlock's precursors, stunted hints of its towering majesty, were without real roots. That was almost 420 million years ago. Tangles of specialized holding branches spread out from the bases of those primordial trunks, across seaweed-covered rocks and into small forests of moss. Some held long enough to allow for change. The idea of the future hemlock was born, bathed in geyser spray and reeking sea gas.

It was the land plants that followed that helped speed the decomposition of the rocks, and it was only then that true soil was born. With soil there could be roots, and only with deep, compounded roots to hold them against the winds could trees grow large. The evolution of the hemlock was assured. It was a time when the rain fell for centuries and raw air superheated by mist-veiled sun and geothermal explosions spawned winds the force of which might stun our senses today. It was a time for giants to be born.

The hemlock had several hundred miles of roots, much of that mass dead woody material, much of it made up of minute single-celled hairlike projections. The root tip itself was hard and consisted of reproducing cells. It was that tip that drove down, snaking past rocks, parting soil, seeking moisture and dissolved minerals. The thin root hairs up behind the tip pushed out to the sides and drank, starting water and minerals on their way to the first leaves 100 feet away. A great deal of the life of the forest lived down there, down where the hard root tip explored for the substances of life and survival in the damp chemical library of soil.

Here dead tissue sloughed off from root tissue containing fixed nitrogen, sugars, amino acids, organic acids, all foods for the minutely small. Concentrations of chemicals exuded from root hairs even as those hairs sucked back minerals and moisture for use aloft. Richly served close to the root itself were bacteria and the spores of the smallest plantlike organisms. The movement of the root through the soil, and of its millions upon millions of hairs, mechanically changed the texture of the matrix, opening channels and compressing others as soil was pushed aside. These capillaries in the earth carried an endless parade of life, all of it happening on a well-balanced scale. Nothing died but that something else might live; nothing lived that something else might not have to die.

The worms were there, earthworms that channeled the soil and aerated it and improved its quality. These silent benefactors of trees and other plants and animals have proved their own perfection by surviving in a world of predator and prey, of storms and drought.

The earthworm is a nocturnal animal. Violently sensitive to white light and dry air, a worm must keep to the dark or at least to the deep shade, and always it must keep itself moist. Moving through the soil along tunnels it has eaten through the mash of organic and inorganic matter, the worm takes in minute animals as well as decaying animal and plant debris. The mass enters through the mouth, or prostomium, and moves along the animal's length. Organic material is absorbed, and mineral debris, gritty matter in the form of casts, leaves through the anus. The transformation of the earthworm's world is thus endless. The worm creates the texture of its environment.

The worms that lived in the forest floor below and near the western hemlock numbered in the hundreds of thousands. A few were seven and even eight years old, for with uncharacteristic good fortune they had escaped their thousand foes. Two patriarchs surfaced near each other under a protective layer of decaying needles and leaves, bacteria, molds, and animal droppings. Sensing each other's presence, they moved closer together until they were side by side, head to tail. Each bore a thickened area called a clitellum; each bore both male and female organs. Strangely, neither could fertilize itself.

Both worms exuded a thick slime that soon encased them; then each contracted, ejecting small quantities of sperm. Minute channels had been left between the slime coat and their bodies, and in these spaces the sperm ran, each worm supplying the other with male cells that would be held viable until the eggs of each were ready to be laid. Once the male sex cells had been exchanged, the worms broke apart and moved away, each to the safety of its own moist burrow. The encounter was brief, its effects eternal upon the species, for by drawing upon each other, they would renew as well as reproduce.

Ten days later the eggs would be ready, and each worm, now distant and forever removed from its partner, would exude slime once again. Only this time the oozing material would form into a ring, and each animal would eject both its own eggs and the sperm cells of the other. Moving away, the worms would leave the sperm to fertilize the eggs and the slime rings to close upon themselves and become true egg cases. Nearly fifty days later two eggs in each case would hatch, the embryos having been nourished by a sticky white substance that had been locked with them in the case as it hardened. Pink and as thin as thread, the young worms would move off to seek their own fortunes in the soil beneath the tree. As each stringling moved, it would feed, and its color would darken from the substances it would absorb from the soil. Each new worm would be a full year away from the time when it could join with another and cross-fertilize as its parents had. It would be a year of feeding, during which the soil would be made better for the worm's having been there.

Once again, as with lichen, nitrogen would be produced by the lowly that all might benefit. As the earthworm digests the organic waste from the tree and its inhabitants, nitrogen forms in the elongated body. The chemical can take many forms, among them ammonia and nitrous acid. The earthworm cannot tolerate these substances for long; any buildup is fatal. In at least 113 of the worm's 117 to 119 segments, there are minute tubules running out to the surface of the animal's body. They are called nephridia, and through them moves a constant flow of urine heavy in nitrogen wastes. Just as the soil is enriched by dripping water carrying newly fixed nitrogen from the lichens 100 feet up in the tree, so does the constantly seeping urine of earthworms carry the same critical element to the soil. Thus the worm feeds the soil upon which it feeds itself.

Many animals eat worms—the smaller snakes, lizards, turtles, moles, shrews, birds, insects—and there are bacterial, fungal, and viral infections that attack them and turn them to jelly. But enough worms are born, four to six from every union, and enough survive to keep rich the debris-laden soil of the forest floor.

Scapanus, the mole, tunneled a foot down below the forest floor. Alone as he would have it, in a rage over his constant hunger, he thrust forward, moving aside 4 yards of soil every hour. With shovel-shaped front feet broader than his hind, he was suited to his life as a minute underground bulldozer. His forelegs and shoulders were enlarged and strengthened, as was his powerful chest. He could do more work in a week than many animals are forced to do in a year. His enormous energy output and his hunger were in balance.

Weighing only 5 ounces, he was yet a powerful factor in the life below the forest floor. He was a hunter.

Stopping to listen, as he did every few seconds, he heard a grating sound nearby. Twitching his naked nose with its upturned nostrils, he angled slightly toward the left. There in the dark world of decay, the worm, too, had sensed its enemy nearby. But the mole was stronger and faster and smarter. With his front legs

The stricken invertebrate convulsed and moved each of its ends in a pointless attempt to escape.

working furiously he pushed ahead, past some pebbles, mountain shards, and buried knots of rotting leaves. The wall separating him from the worm was thin now, and like a prehistoric monster somehow shrunken in size, he burst through the last fraction of an inch of soil and grabbed the worm in the middle of its body. The stricken invertebrate convulsed and moved each of its ends in a pointless attempt to escape. While the worm still lived, the mole chewed until his prey was soft enough to swallow in convulsive gulps. The mole had forty-four teeth in his tiny jaws, more than enough for the task. Far from the sun and the eagle in the tree, the earthworm died, but it did not matter. Its eggs had been laid, and it had fertilized another of its kind as well. The soil and the mole had been served. The worm was not needed now that there would be others to take its place.

The mole, too, had his enemies, and he was destined to feed only a few more times before an animal even smaller than himself would end his life. *Sorex*, the shrew, metabolizes food like an atomic reactor. Eight hours without nourishment are enough to starve the little animal to death. Snuffling after other animals beneath the vegetable debris of the forest floor, it seeks food constantly and will attack animals larger than itself, even others of its kind if too many hours pass between meals. Its world is one of almost constant rage. Were such an animal ever to achieve the size of a hunting hound, it would be the most destructive four-legged vertebrate on earth.

Some hours after *Scapanus* had eaten the worm and

then some beetle grubs, he tunneled upward to avoid a buried rock that seemed too large to go around. *Sorex*, a female carrying young within her, heard the disturbance beneath where she had stopped for a moment. She moved aside slightly to assess the potential. Slowly the mole moved upward, until his head emerged from the soil beneath a blanket of vegetable matter inches deep. *Sorex* chittered in frequencies far too high for human ears and leaped at her prey. The front cluster of her thirty-two teeth fixed behind the mole's skull, in the lethal place at the base where the spine emerges. The two animals were not matched in weight, but what the mole is to the worm the shrew is to the mole. They rolled over and over in the leaves, creating a disturbance that could be sensed for yards around. The mole was soon dead, and the shrew was feeding with urgency, ravening in her hunger. She had not fed for almost an hour. Still chittering in the highest ranges, she ripped at the mole and devoured it in tiny gulps. Although her eyesight was of little use, she looked up several times. She listened well, for the shrew, too, can be surprised and eaten. No predator lives that cannot become prey. In time, almost all do.

The tree's debris and the waste of the plants and animals the tree supported had fed the worm, and the worm, in turn, had helped feed the tree. The worm had fed the mole as well, and the mole the shrew. Still, the eagle sat and waited, and the war below, the shifting of chemicals, the battle for their possession, went on.

6

The tangle of microscopic life that lived within a few millimeters of each of the hemlock's root hairs was a jungle unto itself, no less a forest than the one in which the hemlock stood. To creatures like the worm, lowly, yet large, all such life was a mash of organic matter to be ingested with the soil. Upon such material the worm lived before it fed the mole that fed the shrew. In quantum leaps the smallest motes of matter reached the life of the largest and became part of it. This flow is called the trophic scale, and it is propelled by the power of the universe itself. The least of the microcreatures in the root hair jungle was now locked into the life of the furious shrew, and it was not to stop there.

A stranger had come to the forest, a visitor from rocky outcroppings just a little farther up the slope.

Crotalus viridis oreganus, he was called, the western rattlesnake. Almost 42 inches long, gray and greenish and rough, this specimen had found no prey for several days. He had slipped over a rocky ledge as the sun had risen and heated the small natural oven where he was coiled. He had kept coming, heading down the hill. With no fresh scents to entice him or turn him away, he had moved through the comfortable midday shade, slipping beneath the forest's understory of vine maple, salmonberry, and devil's club. Now he moved into the denser shade of the hemlock and Douglas fir stand. It was moist and quiet, and there were fresh smells, so he began to cast about. Ceaselessly his tongue moved in and out, the tiny holders in its twin tips snatching particles of air, bits of scent, and delivering them to organs in the roof of his mouth. In a way we cannot really understand, he tasted the air, smelled it, too, and came to know its chemistry to an exquisite degree. His awareness was akin to our own in some small ways, but far more acute. For although a dangerous adversary, he was also vulnerable.

Nearby a larger animal unseen by the rattlesnake moved, and instantly the crawling one reacted. Although deaf to airborne waves of sound, the snake, full out and in contact with the ground, could sense the disturbance. *Cervus elaphus*, the elk passing nearby, was 1,000 pounds heavy, and his vibrations were easy to detect. But the giant moved off, and the snake held his S-shaped striking posture for only another minute before relaxing and going his own way. As always, he had been alert and ready to defend himself, but it suited him better that there had been no showdown, no need to fight and risk his fragile life.

The venom that seeped slowly and constantly into small chambers in the glands at the rear of the snake's upper jaw had evolved from saliva. It had taken millions of years to perfect. Its primary purpose was food getting. Rich in digestive enzymes, like all saliva, it helped the snake stop the flight of fast-moving prey and, simultaneously, began that prey's digestion, even before it died. Only to a minor degree did the venom work on the nervous system of prey animals; its principal target was blood. It was designed to destroy blood tissue and the tissues of the system that carry blood within the animal the snake might choose to eat.

But venom has a secondary use in the relatively few snakes that have it. It can be a means of defense. The rattlesnake had not rattled at the first sign of the elk, but had the disturbance increased, the snake's tail would have begun its frenzied movement. The rattle would have been heard. It would have become the snake's first line of defense. Instinctively a snake would rather hold its venom than waste it on things it cannot eat, so first it rattles to tell beasts like elk and man to move away. It is usually only when that signal fails that the rattlesnake will strike out and inject enough venom to warn the intruder off at a second and higher level of defense. Snakes strike when the whole picture drawn by their combined senses convinces them there is no other choice. It is on such a reflex level that fang use is born.

Still, in one out of four strikes a rattlesnake will not use venom at all. It will rely on the stinging sensation of a *dry* bite to warn the foe of what a rattlesnake can really do. If seriously challenged, though, if injured or teased or badly frightened, the always nervous rattlesnake will deny its natural urge to conserve its fluids and inject a heavy dose of venom, enough, at times, to kill rather than warn its enemies.

The elk had not seen the snake, had not really threatened it, so the encounter had come to nothing. The snake was soon hunting again, searching for prey he could kill with purpose, prey that could help him sustain life. He could eat only what he could swallow whole.

In time the rattlesnake came to the area beneath the hemlock upon which the eagle sat. There was too much growth below the eagle's roost for the bird to see the snake, for indeed she might have considered him a handy, if minor, meal. No snake is a match for an eagle coming in swiftly from on high; none can counter the closing talons striking at 80 miles an hour like hammers equipped with rotating knives.

Undetected, the snake came to an evergreen huckleberry bush and pulled himself in to wait and watch and see what the moist forest floor would offer. Like the eagle, he was programmed to wait. He hunted equally well in either mode.

Sorex, after she had finished ripping the mole apart and gulping the pieces down, had begun to hunt again. In the time it would take her to locate a fair meal she would be hungry once more. She moved about frenetically underneath the leaves, snuffling and pushing debris aside. An occasional grub or slug was revealed, and she knew which of these was sweet and which too sour to slay and eat. But they were tiny snacks for the shrew's fierce metabolism.

A shrew's eyesight is not good, for its eyes are extremely small in relation to its skull and suited only to things in close. So the compass of the shrew's world is small, and although it may be frightened by the vibrations of grander forces within its world, it cannot perceive them.

The odor of the shrew is distinctive and well known to rattlesnakes. While not an impressive meal for a large snake, the shrew is warm-blooded and, as protein, entirely acceptable. The snake sensed the disturbance in the leaves nearby and employed special organs in the roof of his mouth, organs known as Jacobson's receptors. Pressing the tips of his tongue into the two cavities there, the snake tasted the shrew at a distance and moved only slightly to be in position to take his meal.

As the meal approached, a second sensing system came into play. Midway between the snake's eyes and external nostril openings lay his heat-sensing pits. That is why his kind are known as pit vipers. Each pit led to two cavities, the larger forward one fed by infrared rays emanating from the shrew. A thin membrane separated the two larger cavities from almost microscopically smaller ones behind. That membrane, rich in nerve endings, measured the heat differential from one side of the snake's head to the other and enabled him to judge his prey's precise position for his bulletlike fang strike. A heat difference of no more than one-fifth of a degree Celsius was enough.

Using both modes—the Jacobson's receptors in his mouth and the infrared radiation entering the cavities in his cheeks—the snake watched the shrew more carefully than the shrew had ever been watched before. When *Sorex* was about 18 inches away, the snake drew back, coil tight upon coil. The spring was charged, and a lifetime of hunting experience would signal the moment of release.

Sorex emerged from behind a small cluster of leaves, barely revealing herself, and a fraction of a second later was rolling over and over in enlarging convulsions. She now contained a substance she had not contained a moment before, a foreign material able to disrupt utterly her entire life system. No power on earth could reverse this explosive chemical shattering of her body. The combined chemistry of the worm, the mole, and the shrew came apart there on the forest floor.

In the instant the shrew had revealed herself, the rattlesnake had tightened one farther inch, moving the top coil only slightly and accentuating the S-shaped curve of the front third of his body. Then he struck. As his head shot forward, his jaws opened so that when they reached the shrew, they would be spread almost 180 degrees. As the upper jaw moved away from the lower, two fangs swung down from their nests on either side and in front of that jaw, and although still almost entirely encased in membranes, they were ready for use. As the snake's perfect strike, guided every millimeter of the way by his heat sensors, reached the shrew, the snake stabbed—he didn't bite, he stabbed, both fangs entering the hot little mammalian body at the same instant. The membranes slid back

along the fangs, and the gleaming and highly specialized teeth sank in a full half inch. Simultaneously the
lower jaw of the snake swung shut, gripping the shrew
on the point of impalement while bundles of muscles
behind the snake's head tightened. The venom moved
quickly along ducts leading forward from each gland
and entering the fangs on top and in front, above the
gum line where the entrance lumina lay. The venom
ran down the fangs and exited through ovoid holes
again on the fangs' leading edges. It then spread out
into tissues of the shrew. She and six unborn young in
her would die convulsively within a minute.

All this had taken less than a second. The snake was
withdrawing from the strike before the first convulsive
shudder ran down the shrew's body. In his withdrawn
S position, the snake now held for an additional moment, then began to relax. The shrew rolled over and
over nearby until, with eyes hardening, jaws agape,
she died. Her young followed in rapid succession, one,
then two until all six had ceased to live. The venom had
reached them through the minutest of blood vessels
connecting them to their mother, had killed them before their mother's own death stopped their lives.

Relaxing still further, the rattlesnake slipped forward
to where the shrew lay stiffening. After nosing his kill,
the snake opened his jaws a second time and posi-
tioned them at the tip of the shrew's nose. He arched
his neck. With incurving teeth fixed on the shrew's
nose, he began moving in the easy and practiced
rhythm of swallowing. In fewer than two minutes the
shrew was a small bulge in the slender part of the

snake's neck. He slipped away then to a fallen log to digest the shrew and her young before attempting to hunt again. Once more some of the chemistry of the tree and the forest floor had changed ownership. A gentle mist fell as the sun was masked by a moving sheet of clouds. The eagle looked out across the tops of lesser trees and in the distance saw a glimmering. There was the sun farther off, and higher up the slope there was snow.

7

A nurse tree on which several younger hemlocks grew was slipping slowly into the soil. It was disintegrating. Weather and the roots of other plants, the action of insects as well, had combined to rend it and free its substance. It had become pulpy and soft, not only a nursery for the young of many kinds but also a home for the aged. Containing animal life in every part, it fed everything from microscopic plants and animals to bears that came to pound and hack at it for the beetles and grubs that tunneled through it.

Many of the animals that live in such a sheltered nest are called thigmotactic. That word describes an animal tropism, a negative or positive incentive, something that attracts or repels a living thing. Light is the basis of two tropisms: the phototropic are attracted by light and move toward it, while the photophobic (the earthworm is an example) move away. Thigmotaxis is such a tropism. It is the desire to be touched on all sides at the same time. Thigmotactic creatures live under bark and under rocks. Often we disturb them and see them frantically scurry to rebury themselves. We assume it is light or temperature or some other force we inflict that worries them. Most often it is not that, but rather a force we have denied them: the force of being touched all over and always at the same time. For that is the force of their comfort and safety. They evolved needing it, for its need meant a higher survival rate.

Many animals are not truly thigmotactic, but at times do seek such security. Under the nurse log, where the roots of four young hemlocks had taken their hold, lived or sometimes just rested many animal forms, all more or less addicted to the tropism of touch.

On the day the rattlesnake came to pay his uncommon visit to the world beneath the hemlock, a creature of great beauty was using the nurse log to comfort himself and hold himself safe—*Lampropeltis zonata*, the exquisite, glossy California mountain king snake. Almost 40 inches long, he lay coiled, quietly resting while faint signals told him it would soon be time to hunt. The rat he had taken four days before had been immature, small, and was all but used up. While not ravening in his hunger, the king snake was close to being stimulated into hunting again. In the meantime, he held his coils, tucked back in against an overhang of undigested log, safely touched and waiting.

The king snake of the California mountains is one of

the most beautiful of all the world's snakes. Shiny and smooth, it has jet black as its first color, over the forward two-thirds of its head. Then comes a narrow band of creamy white, then one of black jet again. A broad band of brilliant red follows, and so it goes the length of the king snake's tubular body: narrow black, narrow cream, narrow black, and broad red. Some people liken it to the coral snake of the South, but no coral snake lives in California, and so no dangerous confusion is possible. The king snake, unlike the coral snake, bears no venom. It is harmless except to the small animals on which it preys.

To the scientist the king snake is in part ophiophagous, an eater of other snakes as well as of mammals and birds. Its generic name, *Lampropeltis*, means "shiny skin." As a group (there are only eight species), the king snakes belong only to the New World and range from Canada to Equador. None is more beautiful than *L. zonata*, the king snake of California's mountains.

Although *L. zonata* may be found at sea level (but never in the desert), they are more common at higher altitudes. They may, in fact, be found as high as 8,000 feet—jewels, chains of glistening, muscular light and color, hunting, resting, and hunting again. The king snake hunts during the daylit hours unless the weather is very hot. Then it will shift its pattern and hunt at night.

On this day he lay coiled not far from where the rattlesnake had taken *Sorex*. The disturbance had not been lost to the king snake. An old and experienced warrior, he knew the vibrations that came to him along the forest floor, and he knew the scents, for his forked tongue, too, flicked in and out to taste the air and learn its offerings and its threats.

The musklike odor of the rattlesnake was easy to detect, and the almost hungry king snake was triggered. The scent had shifted the balance, and now he was ready to eat—to hunt and *then* to eat. The taste of the rattlesnake on the air was no less than would be the smell of a steak on the grill or a cake in the oven to a human nose. The king snake uncoiled, stretched out flat, and started out tight in where the flaking undercurve of the log met the debris-strewn floor. Guided by the intensity of smell and by the vibrations transmitted through the ground, he moved toward an intersecting path. Extended straight out in order to keep close to the log and in the gray light of the falling mist, the king snake gleamed like a rope of gems more than 3 feet long. In fact almost 2 inches shorter than the rattlesnake, he would still cast the challenge when they met. He was immune to rattlesnake venom and could thus afford the chance. He might be driven off by a frenzied defense of some sort, but he could not be killed by an animal whose only real weapon was an injectable chemical.

The king snake remained hidden during the period of the rattlesnake's hunt, kill, and feeding. Only when the rattlesnake moved away to coil beneath a bush did the gleaming hunter begin to stalk his meal.

As the king snake had located the rattler through his powers of chemoreception, the rattler now used the same means to detect the mounting danger. Within minutes of the rattlesnake's coming to rest, the two hunters faced each other with eyes that could not blink and lips that could neither smile nor express fear or pain.

The rattlesnake feared the king snake by instinct and therefore did not assume the normal defensive striking coil or S shape. Instead, he pushed his aftercoils against the stem of the bush under which he had

The rattlesnake again turned the center of his body into

crawled, thereby to gain leverage for a backward twin-
ing retreat, and pressed his head and the front third of
his body against the ground. His nervous pitch had
peaked in the first few seconds of awareness, and now
his tail buzzed angrily. The king snake moved forward
slightly and then did a strange thing. Coiling loosely,
he began to vibrate his tail as well. Resting as it did
among some leaves, the tip set up a buzz not unlike
that of the rattlesnake's horny tail. The two snakes an-

a looped club and raised it to swing down again.

swered each other's warning *whrrrring,* although neither could hear. It was a strange reflexive mute play in the forest's understory gloom. The king snake buzzed his false rattle sound for only a moment, then pressed on, for the rattlesnake was pulling away, writhing backward over a fallen branch. The king snake followed until the rattler was pressed back tight against a large log, unable to get over it without raising his head off the ground. And this the rattler was unwilling to do. It would be the head the king snake would try to grasp to begin swallowing.

The king snake came within a foot of the rattlesnake before the venomous one made his first truly defensive move. Instead of striking out, as he would have done against any other animal that threatened him, the rattler looped the middle third of his heavy, roughly scaled body and raised it high over his head. Then he slithered forward, and instantly the heavy coil of his tense and threatened body struck the ground near the king snake's head. The king snake pulled back as the rattlesnake again turned the center of his body into a looped club and raised it to swing down once more.

Over and over the rattlesnake's body thumped to the ground, once striking the king snake a glancing blow to the head when he failed to withdraw in time. Each time the king snake backed off. In what he had inherited within the substance of his egg was the certain knowledge that his patience was greater, that he could outwait the rattlesnake. His prey would tire. The king snake expended almost no energy at all. The rattler was exhausting himself with his lashing attack. His only hope was that the king snake might beome intimidated and move away. This the glistening warrior was not about to do. He had met too many rattlesnakes in his life, and only when he had been very small had the danger of a battered skull driven him away. As a large snake he had come to accept his supremacy and take his hysterical prey with cold-eyed efficiency.

Within minutes the rattler had indeed worn himself down, and the lashing coil fell less frequently to earth before the king snake's nose, and with less conviction. Having been struck only once, and that a minor blow, the king snake was undeterred. He moved back and forth, in and out, drawing, yet avoiding the thumping punishment of the rattlesnake's nonchemical defense.

Nearby, on the other side of the nurse log, there sat another stranger to this part of the forest. Having pushed aside the log's rotting wood in search of grubs, *Euarctos americanus*, the American black bear, was sitting back on his haunches and munching on the treasure hoard he had uncovered. He listened as the rattlesnake's coil struck the ground again and again. Unable to see the action nearby, from time to time he pointed his muzzle straight to the sky and wrinkled his nose. He snuffled and sniffed, for like all bears, he believed only his nose. Deciding that there would be time enough to investigate, he went back to his grubs, making sucking sounds over the joy of their texture and their slightly sharp taste. His long claws flaked away layers of tree growth, now pulped free of many structural chemicals, in order to expose more of the unformed insects. He would finish here first, before looking into whatever was taking place no more than two dozen feet away.

His claws flaked away layers of tree growth — He would finish here first.

Hundreds of feet above all this, the eagle sat waiting for the signal that would tell her to kick free again and seek her own meal. Again she looked up the slope to where snow was melting, sending rivulets down toward the relatively level floor of the coniferous stand where the hemlock grew.

The rattlesnake was tired now. Two dozen times he had raised his looped body and cast it toward the king snake only to strike the hard ground. As the moving target of the king snake had drawn him out, the debris underneath the rattlesnake had become more unsettled. His only fixed point of contact was his chin on the forest floor. He slithered back and forth but did not relinquish that one hold on safety. Touch, contact, is always important to a snake. At a moment of extreme peril it is more important than ever.

The king snake's instincts triumphed. The resolve of the rattlesnake finally dissipated. No matter where he pushed and coiled the enemy was always there, blocking him. A rattlesnake deprived of the use of his venom, and instinctively aware of that fact, can be worn down easily. The king snake knew this with his own instincts, taught by time and the million rattlesnakes taken by his ancestors, and when the moment was right, he rushed. Like a gleaming arrow, he struck and had the rattlesnake's usually deadly head in his front teeth. He coiled around the venomous one and constricted. The rattlesnake could not fill his lungs, and soon his heart stopped beating. Working back and forth, hinged in front and at the center, the king snake's bottom jaw worked over the broader span of his lance-headed prey. Although in death he still lashed and coiled in one ineffective move after another, the rattlesnake was soon on his way down toward the pool of powerful digestive juices within the king snake, juices that would break down not only the snake but also the shrew the snake had eaten, and the mole, and the worm, and the microscopic mash that had fed the worm.

The bear snuffled up over the log, tired of beetles and their grubs and curious about the disturbance nearby. The eagle tipped forward, for now she sensed the bear. But there was no meal there, nothing the eagle could challenge and kill. *Kya*, her falsetto rang out, *kya, kya, kya.*

8

The black bear was no more than a some-time visitor to the tall coniferous forest. Around the forest's edges, and in other areas nearby where the sun more easily reached the earth, grew stands of blackberry bushes, and these the bear would visit when he was in the vicinity. Often he was on his way to or from the higher slopes, where the snow lasted longer and the meadows were cool. He could dig out ground squirrels and nibble on grasses and sedge in such places.

When his transits to the alpine flats and through the rich berry-bush growth took him by the coniferous stands, he would move into the shade and nap, or he would seek a stump or log to pull apart for beetles and other insects. A bear is omnivorous and may graze like a cow one day, browse like a deer the next, and on the third day pull down a deer like his distant cousin the wolf. Bears take bee grubs as well as honey, and they take carrion—any protein to mix with the vegetable matter they are constantly ingesting. From spring into fall, bears eat, putting on thick layers of fat against the winter, when most of them eat not at all.

The bear does not hibernate. It does den up, often under windfalls and rotten logs, but often, too, under grassy slopes where its tunnel can open to the north. Southern exposure could mean the entrance of intermittently melting snow and a water-soaked den. Facing the north, a den entrance is soon blocked by more reliable snow, which then hardens from wind and constant chill. Behind that wall the bear sleeps until it is warm again—but it does not hibernate, for its body temperature and heart rate stay nearly normal. A bear may be awakened at any time and may even wander through the snow before returning to sleep again. But during the spring, summer, and fall months the bear builds fat.

The bear that had come to the hemlock stand for a spicy meal of insect grubs shuffled over toward the spot where the king snake and the rattler had met. His gait was rolling, and his hanging head swung from side to side. His eyes were slow to find the evidence, but his nose had taken him to the right area, and his ears had helped as well. By the time the bear found the source of the disturbance the king snake had more than a foot of the rattlesnake inside him. He was working himself along over his prey, which was larger than he was. Once again a hunter had himself become prey, his ultimate fate determined not as a matter of style, but in terms of the substances he held in trust while he lived. If the style of a life is technique, its substance is chemistry. Technique dies when an animal realizes a few abrupt changes inside itself, like the stopping of a beating heart or the failure of oxygen to circulate, grasped in the iron or copper of its blood. The technique can die, but the chemicals cannot. They must go on.

The bear sat back on his haunches. He weighed more than 450 pounds, and his rump did not have far to go. Whenever he shifted his position, his long black coat flowed, settling down in rippling waves. The bear watched the king snake struggle with his massive prey. The gleaming jewel snake was trapped by his meal. Unable to regurgitate the full foot he had eaten, he was locked to the place where he had made his kill until such time as he could swallow it all, and even then he would not be able to move very far off until at least some of it had been digested.

After a few minutes the bear grunted forward onto his four pillar legs. He walked over to the two snakes locked in what was to have been a death struggle for just one of the two. The king snake knew the bear was there but could not crawl away. Desperately he tried to rid himself of the meal that had trapped him, but before he could mount a second convulsive attempt to regurgitate the rattler, the bear's paw was there.

Like most animals, bears are cautious with snakes. They may kill them, even eat them, but they are cautious. The king snake and the rattlesnake were lifted up and sent flying, hooked into the air with a single swipe of the giant's paw. They fell to earth upside down, and the king snake struggled to right himself, still held against his will by the rattlesnake still rippling reflexively. Finally, by coiling and twisting, the king snake righted himself and his meal. But once again the two snakes were sent flying through the air. They struck a tree, and now the king snake was too badly injured to survive. The bear approached the snake tangle and raked his paw across first one snake, then the other. Both snakes opened; their entrails were exposed. The eyes of the king snake were bleak as death approached; his jaw was agape; his tongue lolled and fetched no more tastes of air. Inside him was the death face of another snake that had died just minutes ago. Once again the bear clawed at the dead and dying snakes, ripping them more, exposing more. As the king snake finally died, he released a slush of musk from his anal opening. The bear sniffed the two dead animals, then rolled on them. Again and again he rolled over them, gaining the smell of their death on his coat. Then he ate a little, first from the rattlesnake and then from the king snake, just a little of each, and then he rolled on them again. It was more ritual than food getting.

As the bear ambled away from what remained of the two dead snakes, one still locked inside the other by a third of its length, both broken and filthy, their blood and entrails mixing with the dead leaves and the fungus and microlife of the forest floor, insects were already scenting what would be a hearty meal. And a shrew, litter mate of the one eaten by the rattlesnake less than an hour before, came forward, up out of the leaves. Carrion is a rich find for anything from a bear to the least of the protein seekers. The dead snakes would not last long on the forest floor. Even the bones would be carried off or broken down. The calcium those bones contained would enrich the lives of many.

The bear left the forest grove. He had stopped by to find some grubs, brought near by berries bursting with juice at the edge of the conifer stand. The episode with the snakes had been more play than anything else. It had been of no serious consequence, just something to do at a time, now in the middle of fall, when the bear was alone and, perhaps, in the way of the bear, a little bored. Since early June he had followed a corpulent sow and had mounted her regularly. In his fierce displeasure at surplus company he had driven off the sow's yearling cub, and although she had bawled threats at first, she had not interfered. Now, though, and for almost another year, he would be alone. He entertained himself by tearing logs apart, often for no more than an ounce or two of beetle grubs, and by games such as killing snakes. The new smell on his coat, a smell that would linger for days, somehow pleased him, and that was enough. The bear was a taker, a mountain of an animal unchallenged in a natural system except by his own kind. He moved beyond the standlings at the edge of the conifer forest. It might be a year or more before he entered such a place again. It was not his usual habitat.

Tuk, tok, tok—metallic, harsh, the raven's voice. *Cuurruucc*, and *tuk, tok, tok* again. The raven had watched the action. Before the bear appeared, he had been close to tackling the feeding king snake himself.

Now he rudely called his displeasure after the lumbering brute. *Tok*, the raven called again, and hopped to a branch closer to the carrion.

The raven is a *Corvus* bird, a relative of the crows, jackdaws, jays, magpies, and the rooks of Europe. It is the smartest of all birds, and the brashest. And it is both adaptable and dangerous to lesser life. A full 2 feet long with its wedge-shaped tail, a raven will take nestlings, eggs, small mammals, reptiles, and amphibians, either living or in the form of carrion. When it has to kill, it uses its heavy bill, pounding straight down in hammerblows that can crush a skull or break a back. Much larger and heavier than its cousin crow, the raven is one of the toughest birds alive.

The bear was well gone when the raven hopped another branch closer. He cocked his head, ruffling the neck feathers that gave him such a goitered look. It seemed safe, it seemed certain, yet the raven called yet another *tok* before hopping to the ground where the snakes lay in their locked death. Cocking his head once again, the raven strutted forward in his raven way, then hopped up to the mangled reptiles. He looked down and pecked, lifting away a mouthful. The shrew that had been approaching moved back judiciously under the leaves, toward the log the bear had ripped away before being distracted by the snake fight. Forgetting the snakes, the shrew scrambled up along the log and feasted on beetles and grubs that still lay exposed, that were still trying to bury themselves again. Meanwhile, the raven fed on the snakes. The bear had left his spoor of destruction; now others would feed.

Near the edge of the conifer stand the bear had stopped and deposited a pile of scats. An inch and a half in diameter and of uniform size, the bear scats contained substances from far up the slope and from other places, too. They were not dirt in this context, just organic matter. Before the bear was out of sight, before the raven had taken its first beakful of snake carrion, beetles were approaching the scats. They, too, the bear had added to the system. Like all organic matter, they would be used. There was no one there to remember the bear, yet his passage could not be forgotten by the forest. He had been joined with it, had become a part of it.

9

Near where the hemlock stood towered a massive Douglas fir, *Pseudotsuga*, the "false hemlock." The two are seen often in association, for the same factors favor the growth of each. This giant was more than four hundred years old and stood 175 feet tall. At its base, near the ground on which it had nursed during its centuries of growth, the bark was almost 2 feet thick, deeply furrowed and very rough. Its great, scarlike ridges were joined irregularly with cross ridges. The tree wore its years with dignity.

The bark of the great fir was dark brown on its outer aspect, where it faced the world, but deep inside, where insects burrowed and other lesser creatures huddled and reproduced in a pageant of life, the bark was a deep red-brown, a clear color whose beauty was a secret from all but a few forms with eyes to see. The bark of this species, a cosmos of many life-forms, varies according to the climate in which the tree has grown. Here, in the moistness of its natal slope, the bark stood thick and firm, lush with health, while on a higher, drier slope it would have been gray and corky.

The foliage of the great Douglas tree was dense and close to yellow-brown. Again, in drier areas the color would have been different, it would have edged over on the scale toward blue-green, and an observer would know this tree had wanted for water for all or much of its life. A tree records its world.

The foliage of the Douglas fir lasts about eight years before it falls away to be replaced by more needles, flat structures, grooved on top and blunt. Only occasionally does this species produce some needles that are sharp and truly pointed.

The cones of this fir are easily distinguished. Maturing in August or at least by September, they are cinnamon and sometimes even more reddish brown than that. They are just over 4 inches long, almost four times as long as those of the true *Tsuga*, the western hemlock, in which the eagle sat. The cones of Douglas fir bear trident bracts that protrude from among the scales that, in turn, hide the seeds. By September those russet seeds with their small white markings are ready to leave the womb of the cone and seek the earth below, where a new tree may incubate and grow.

In and around the fir another world existed, a world kept secret from us, for we do not have the means to detect it. Its endless action is for instruments more finely tuned than those we have thus far been able to evolve or perhaps retain. Indeed, it would seem that we are moving away from this awareness that ties so much of the natural world together: the savory awareness of smell.

The animals, the greatest and the least of them included, that passed the way of the Douglas fir and its associated growth left signals, produced signs, and engaged in airborne social gestures. A bobcat that had ventured by two days earlier had rubbed his face against a rough place on the tree's bark and secreted a minute quantity of fluid. We would call the action scratching, and although, indeed, the simple act may have felt good to the cat, he was doing much more than serving a momentary need for comfort. He was telling other cats, males that might seek to crowd his hunting space or females that might find him intriguing, that a great male had come that way. He had marked the tree as his own. He had spoken clearly with scent.

It seems certain that the first signal ever given by a living organism was a chemical one, a substance we now call a pheromone. The earliest bacteria that twisted through the earliest sea called to each other in this way. It is believed that pheromones, the elements of that first vocabulary, remain the fundamental source of communication for most kinds of living creatures today.

In most species pheromones are sex attractants, but not always that alone. Where they do serve that purpose, though, they are powerful, pervading, electrifying to those creatures equipped to receive the message.

Among the beetles, butterflies, moths, and ants that lived in the associated forest of hemlock and spruce and fir, the pheromones not only signaled that females had ripened but very often contained an aphrodisiac that drove the males on, forcing them to abandon all other goals and seek their real purpose in the source of the smell. In such creatures, responding to the overwhelming scent of ripeness, sex is not a pleasure but a consuming compulsion that death alone can still. Pheromones do not taunt and tempt; they command.

The pheromones that swirled around the great Douglas fir served a parade of forms, not only the animals of a single species. They advertised other compulsions that were interspecific in importance. Science has given the name *allomone* to scents when the boundary of species is crossed. The allomones, too, played their role.

Ants frequently assign a double role to their chemical language. Soldiers seeking targets for massed attack lay down pheromones as we might unwind a ball of string in a maze of mine shafts. They form an invisible avenue of odor that guides any of their kind along the same trail. When the target is located, the ants send messengers back. As they approach the hoards of their own kind, they discharge a stronger scent, and the rally begins. The pheromones excite the hungry, which then stream out, following the chemical trail the original scouts lay down. As the hapless victims are approached, the ants in the lead again discharge their minute scent signals, and a double purpose is served. As pheromones the signals further excite the attackers to abandon all caution—to serve the greater good and die without hesitation if necessary. As allomones the same signals, perhaps some slightly enhanced, throw those being attached into panic and weaken their resolve to resist. Some ants eat those they take, and others carry their captives off as slaves, but the network of signals is unending, and the war continuous. There are no calls to arms, no voices, and few gestures in the madness of the assault. But there is a stream of chemical signals, a primordial language still in use.

Deer carry at least seven sources of pheromones with which to facilitate their society. Their feces and urine, materials strangely wasted in our social connections, contain pheromones to be read by all others of their kind. Other scents are discharged by tarsal and metatarsal glands from two positions on their hind legs. Glands on their foreheads and under their eyes enable them to mark sites just as the bobcat did. Deer also carry glands between their toes and near their tails. Some of the signals sent by the deer are airborne, and some are meant to be rubbed on marking places. Each scent has a different purpose in a whole language of smell to which we remain oblivious.

We hear crickets chirp and know the males are rubbing their forewings together. We often forget the male will do that only when females discharge a pheromone that signals the male it is time to "sing" of cricket love.

In water a chemical signal has ten thousand times the life-span of a scent released in air. Similarly, it takes ten thousand times as long for a chemical in water to reach the limits of its range without benefit of the draft and eddy and rush of wind. As a corollary of these two facts, it takes a million times as much scent material in water as in air to achieve the same purpose. But the system that makes trees grow and eagles fly has solved that mathematical offset, too. Proteins are involved in scent particles intended for the world of water. In air, scent is dispersed by vapor pressure, and even when the air is calm, the small molecular structure of the pheromone allows it to disperse rapidly and reach its target in time for the signal to serve its purpose. Protein molecules are heavier, more grossly structured, and, unless taken up by dust particles or water droplets, will not perform their function well in air. They are perfect for the world submerged, however, and that is where they do their work. All waterborne pheromones known to us contain a large percentage of protein molecules.

In every droplet, in every small accumulation of water beneath the great spreading trees, the protein molecules float back and forth, drawing and driving each species in the functions of its life and society. In the air above and around the trees, millions of higher animals—ascending from invertebrates to the mighty cats and the deer tribe—spray and rub their world with pronouncements of intent, purpose, and need.

Among no animals, though, is scent more highly re-fined than among insects and their kin. A female spider (an arachnid and not an insect, though still an ar-thropod) leaves a single silken strand drenched with scent, and this the hapless male has to follow. Un-equipped with a penis, he can only spin a sperm web when he comes to the end of his quest, and onto this web he discharges his contribution to the next generation and to his species. Using an especially adapted appendage, he next lifts drops of his own fluid and inserts them into the enchantress, the silk spinner he has blindly followed. The female waits patiently. In some species she may turn away in seeming disdain when the job is done, while in others she turns and eats the male. There will be no struggle.

Moths, the kinds that flew between the hemlock and the Douglas fir, release perhaps the most incredible pheromones of all. Some species are equipped to respond to one eighty-trillionth of an ounce in a gallon of neutral fluid. Some males respond to microscopic quantities of scent over a distance of 5 miles.

For all this seeming excellence of the pheromonic world there are handicaps. A scream can change in pitch, a purr may become a hum, and a grimace a gentler mien, but the chemical signals in the forest are more rigid and far more difficult to orchestrate. Once sent, these signals cannot be recalled. Their advantages, though, are obvious. They can be transmitted during hours of light or darkness and are affected by neither. They can find their way around all obstacles. They are extremely efficient from the point of biological strength, for all they require is an open pore or an exposed surface. They can be detected at greater distances than any other signal produced by most animals (although whales surely have greater vocal range in the sea). The pheromones of the myriad forest species are long-lasting and are apparently not subject to misinterpretation. They are readily broadcast into the future. The elk that passed by the hemlock and the bobcat that stopped to rub his cheek against the Douglas fir did not need to know when the next of its kind would pass that way. They signaled blindly ahead and rested certain of the results.

The sky above the forest had been an unsettled gray for several hours. Brilliant sunshine had given way to slivers of clouds—fingers, at first, then streamers—and the quality of light failed minute by minute while the amount of moisture in the air, even at the level of tree trunk and branch, increased. There was a drop in temperature, too, as water gathered up over the Pacific days before it moved toward the east, turning the sky into a great gray sponge. On the western face of the mountains, over slopes where snow and ice were seldom absent, the air cooled, and the water that had been vapor became liquid once again. It began running down the creviced trunks of trees even before it began falling from the sky. The wind rose, the sky became darker yet, and in the far distance the thunder rolled in. Muffled at first, it became sharper and more assertive.

The first bolts of lightning flashed against the gray. Blistering, jagged streaks of light carried energy from polarity to polarity in a heavily charged sky. The lightning came first, and then the thunder, as sound and light traveled at their different speeds. When it was close, the thunder cracked like a giant rock exploding, and then there would be a distant answer muted by sheets of rain and intervening peaks.

The falling water was driven down and across. It lashed into the forest and swept needles and leaves

The falling water was driven down and across — each drop fell as an exploding bomb.

from living trees and birds from branches, where they hunkered in fear. Even larger animals moved nervously into more sheltered places. The drops of rain that could be gentle and warming on a summer day now stung and chilled, and some birds died. Each drop fell as an exploding bomb. One drop in a tiny sea on a curled leaf or tree crevice could totally disrupt everything that lived there—jarring, scattering, changing, stunning. The vast concerto of pheromones became a world of disharmony as signals were joined in running streams and the floor of the forest became a temporary lake. Debris floated and washed and slushed against standing things. A mole turned in its hole and started to dig deeper as streams of water began fingering down the tunnel behind it. Worms somehow alerted to the moister and darker world the forest had become began angling upward to where later many would be eaten.

Probably millions of microscopic and near-microscopic animals died in the fury of the passing storm. Insects, slime molds torn apart, arachnids, egg cases, nests, webs, bodies—all dashed, scattered, churned into the soup the rain became as it reached the forest floor. Some species would be favored by the excessive moisture; others harmed. It was all part of a balance that would even out with future events as it had with past.

So the Pacific Ocean contributed more of its substance, made salt-free by its journey through the systems of the sky to the forest. The storm came for good or ill, each species to measure the effect by its own standards. It passed from the forest as yellow light, of nuclear rather than electric origin, began fingering its way through the gray. Soon the electric force, the lightning, and its offspring thunder were across the ridge, still carrying on but in a different place. They had visited the forest and were gone. Once again the animal life there began laying down its signals, marks, summonses, advice, and instructions. The pheromonic world would repair itself.

As the storm rolled across the nearest peaks, an exotic stranger to the western forests emerged from a hollow log and shook himself. With a confused look on his unintelligent-appearing face, he began to amble across a sodden clearing toward a tall deciduous stand that had managed to survive the crowding evergreens that dominated that part of the wood. A noise, though, caught his attention, and he turned, appeared even more confused than before, and shuffled back into the log from which he had emerged. He squatted down inside and waited. He would try again to get across to the leafy trees beyond.

It was part of a saga, the appearance in the forest of the Virginia opossum. He was the first of his kind to reach this stand, and if the pattern of his ancestors was to hold, he would become a common sight—his mates and progeny, and their mates and progeny.

Nowhere on earth are marsupials natively common except in the southern Americas, Australia, and New Guinea. They are primitive mammals that produce no placenta and give birth to embryonic young. But centuries ago the opossum began a northward migration from somewhere in South America. The species that appeared that day after the storm had passed reached Mexico long before the first Europeans ever touched the shores of the New World. Later in the same prehistoric period it reached the landmass that would eventually be called the United States of America. Its earliest contacts with scientifically minded Europeans was in what was soon to be called Virginia, so the animal became known as *Didelphis virginiana*, and the name stuck for more than two hundred years. Only very recently has it changed, and today, in Mexico and the United States, it is *Didelphis marsupialis*, and there is no longer confusion about its range.

After Europeans settled in the new land, the opossum continued its march. It was found in New England and then well into southern Canada. At some point someone packed specimens into a crate, and the march of the opossum from the jungles of South America was aided by roaring jet planes. The species was released in California, where it is now a common animal. It spread out and covers much of the state's 155,000 square miles and is found in Washington and Oregon as well. Forest by forest, grove by grove, it has progressed, and that is a monumental achievement when the odds against it are considered.

Opossums generally are slow-witted, easy prey for eagles, canine and feline hunters, and automobiles. Millions die on roads and in the jaws of predators, and in the United States alone more than three million are trapped each year for their low-quality fur. Yet the opossum—ill-tempered, dull-witted, slow, and confused—still manages not only to hold on but to increase and spread. It is a successful species, although it gives a contrary impression.

The single male animal that came to the forest and outstayed the storm would be followed by a female. They would mate the following spring, and within thirteen days a litter of five to sixteen would appear. That is the shortest gestation period of any mammal in North America. At birth each infant would weigh 1/7,000 pound. At the moment of birth its own saga would begin. The ill-formed embryo must crawl through its mother's fur until it reaches a nipple. It must claim that nipple, take it into its mouth, and wait for it to swell. From then on the infant nurses on what has become not only its source of nourishment but its anchor.

Sixty days pass before the young's eyes open, and by that time it must have increased its body weight five hundred times if it is to survive detachment from its mother at the age of three months, in another thirty days. At one year the baby is mature enough to venture off. It can live six more years, but few, if any, opossums make it. There are too many accidents waiting to happen, too many eager predators waiting to feed. The opossum survives as a species because it bears so many young while still young itself. It defeats its enemies in the same way it feeds them: by numbers.

The opossum waited in the log. At dusk he would try again. If he were to die, it would not matter to the forest. Others would come. They always do once the first opossum appears. The march of their kind from the jungled river bottoms of South America has been an inexorable force. The fact that jet planes and shipping crates have helped along the way is nothing more than a mechanical detail. The opossum would have come anyway. One thing that does not bother the opossum at all is time. Millions of years have passed, and millions more are to come. Through it all the dim-witted marsupials move forward, the only direction for them to go.

10

 One of the most peculiar sequences of events that took place regularly in the moist soil and rotting vegetation beneath the tall trees happened on a scale that mocks human vision. Where water remained after the rainstorm, in a curled leaf or indentation on a rotting log, slime molds developed.

In the early stages there appeared to be nothing more than a large number of amoebas living free of each other as single-celled animals. But at some point—and no one knows the exact signal—there came a call. The amoebas swarmed. They pushed toward each other, bunching up like an unruly mob, and suddenly, where there had been thousands of free-swimming microscopic creatures, there was a single form of many cells. It did not stop there.

The mass of cells began to take on a plantlike appearance, something like a miniature toadstool. As the slime mold took this alternative form, a long stalk grew up, and a single glistening drop appeared at its tip like a tiny jewel. It was a jewel of life, for within this minute container were lodged thousands of spores, each with a destiny as profound and as mysterious as those of the hemlock and the fir. The shimmering gem was a fruiting body. At a certain point it exploded, and the spores were released into the drops of water where the colony had taken hold. Each spore, in turn, quickly changed into an amoeba, one like those that had massed and created the fruiting body in the original transformation.

Each spore that was cast free from the jewel had an outer layer that was very much like the cellulose of a tree. There was an inner layer of slime. As each spore split, the emerging amoeba began to hunt almost immediately. It sought bacteria, surrounding its prey one at a time. It incorporated their matter into itself. The bacteria in the tiny sea could not last long against the hordes, and soon there were only amoebas. Each grew as it fed, but when there was too little to eat and all were about to perish, when the food in the microsea was used up, another transformation began.

First, the amoebas began to shrink, and then some of them—again, it is a mystery how they are selected—discharged a chemical called acrasin. The substance spread out through the water like a chemical magnet, and no amoeba sensing its message would ever be quite the same again. The amoeba hordes began to swarm toward those centrally situated pipers. Soon they were touching them, sticking to them, almost becoming a part of them. The responders, too, began to secrete acrasin, and other amoebas responded to that. The puddle that only minutes before had swarmed with free-living, hunting amoebas was now a watery desert except for the mass that had come into being. The amoebas formed themselves into a body that some people liken to a minute garden slug. It was covered with slime and left a slime trail behind as it moved. The amoebas retained their identity. Each was an individual animal, but they had massed to avoid death and to migrate.

Over a period of hours the sluglike mass of amoebas moved—toward warmth, toward moisture, toward food. During the move there was a constant changing of position within the slimy sausage. Some amoebas died by the wayside, slipping out from the envelope that contained the whole. Others pushed ahead, forcing the rest to rush to stay attached. The churning was ceaseless, but the slime body stayed intact.

Eventually this mold sausage found a suitable place for its next phase. A stalk began to form at one end. Some cells contributed the celluloselike matter that formed this stalk; others massed to form the spores in the new fruiting body. The spores slipped free of the top of the stalk and fell to earth where it was warm and moist. They soon looked much like all the other amoebas in the soil, but this was an illusion. Inside each was the code, the ability to respond to chemical signals other amoebas could not hearken to. It would be just a matter of time before the amoebas massed and began their incredible cycle again. If the water droplets they had come upon became too barren of prey, they would migrate once more.

The slime mold formation and migration had occurred billions of times beneath the great trees during their years of growth. The bacteria eaten by the amoebas and the matter they supplied to other minute hunters—all were part of the system. Every drop of water, every dent in every leaf and branch and fallen log was a jungle submerged. Life swarmed there as it did everywhere. The rich broths of mighty trees in a moist climate, where mists often come in over high ridges and blanket the trees from top to forest floor, are suited to these cycles. And for each one we know of there are surely a thousand more.

The bacteria hunted by the amoebas in the small pools of water and in the thin sheets of moisture that separated the particles of soil were themselves of almost infinite variety. Some were pathogenic or parasitic; they invaded other organisms, some not much larger than themselves and others billions of times their own weight, and destroyed them by secreting toxins that caused disease. Some, though, were nonpathogenic or saprophytic. They could live on organic and inorganic matter. Some formed what we often call mildew, before disintegrating into pools of degraded organic matter.

The myriad forms of bacteria that squirmed their microscopic paths through the soil were chemical missionaries. They worked full time at conversion. They took the chemicals they found and changed them, over and over until they were fit for use by other forms of life. Proteins attacked by bacteria decomposed into polypeptides and from that formed into complex amino acids. The acids in turn became ammonia. The residue in decomposing organic matter left after the extraction of the amino acids became carbon dioxide and water. While some bacteria created ammonia, others took the ammonia, extracted its nitrogen, and created other substances of use to green plants.

These smallest organisms played a vital part in the soil composition of the forest. To them was assigned the role of circulation. They took the debris and reduced it to atoms of carbon, nitrogen, and sulfur, as had been their task since life began. Without bacteria in the soil, life as we know it would be far different. Perhaps it could not go on at all.

In these fields of swirling green and purple bacteria, and some of other colors, too, the amoebas hunted. But the food supply was constant. The bacteria maintained their infinite numbers by simply dividing into two, each mother becoming two daughter cells.

Whereas the spiders and the insects that live in and around the trees of the conifer forest number in the millions, the lesser lives, the chemical circulators, number in the billions. A spoonful contains a cosmos. The chain of life began there, not only because that is the level at which the essential chemical conversions took place but also because that is where the smallest prey were to be found. The amoeba took the bacterium, the worm the amoeba, and so it began, to end with the bear and other animals that came to the forest—and, of course, the tree.

The rich mash of the pine forest offered many opportunities for many takers. The mushrooms thrived. *Peziza*, lilac shading to tan, worked with the others to reduce wood to pulp and pulp to absorbable liquid of great complexity. There were the pallid, saucer-shaped *Discina*, the large, rubbery, smoky brown *Sarcosoma*, and the pale brown *Neournula* looking like small urns from a distant culture. The wine red to purple *Helvella* mushroom clustered over rotting logs, along with the dull reddish brown saddle-cupped *Gyromitra*. All of them worked as the insects worked—reducing, recycling, flourishing with dead things killed by other causes. Some fungi are sweet to the taste and safe as well, others are more bland, and many are deadly, lashing the gut, twisting it in savage convulsions that can end only in death. Man must be taught one from the other. Lesser animals know.

For the nervous red fox that came often to the coniferous forest, mushrooms were a minor relish. The bright coppery little dog came to hunt and scavenge after a variety of foodstuffs from berries to voles, from insect grubs to reptiles and amphibians. The most omnivorous of North American canids, the fox will take what it can find. It is a shy animal because it crosses trails left by wolves, coyotes, and big cats. Any of those larger, more aggressive carnivores, if hungry enough, will kill and eat a fox. Being a predator is no guarantee an animal will not become prey. The wit of the small predator must bear two edges for each day it hopes to survive.

Carefully, on dainty, high-stepping feet, the fox

moved among the trees and brush, nose to the ground. Among the soft pale green of the ferns his color showed brighter yet. It was the gentlest of palettes. When shafts of sunlight from the cathedral tops of the forest found him, dappled him in ferns taller than he was, it was like the inspired idea of a fine artist.

Though a solitary animal, the fox engaged in a strange social interplay with others of his kind. Not comfortable in the company of other foxes, except when it was time to mate, he nevertheless interacted with his species in the constant transmission of signals. Not only did these signals reward his own feeding efforts, but with them he also helped other foxes he seldom saw in their quest for food. The medium of communication was urine.

A fox may mark with urine as many as seventy locations within a single hour, a feat almost impossible for a primate to contemplate. Again we glimpse the miraculous world of pheromones. Each urine marking is a clear message. If a fox finds food with a low odor potential, one unlikely to attract another fox after he has eaten it, no urine mark is deemed necessary. But if a fox happens on food with a powerful scent, a decaying carcass, for example, one whose liquid remnants or stain will continue to send forth attractive odors even after the real substance has been consumed, the fox will urinate there. That tells the next fox that comes along not to hunt for a meal; it has been used up. Only if the urine mark is weak and the remnant scent of the vanished food particularly strong will the second fox ignore the message and continue to hunt.

In this strange way, communicating with animals all but strangers to him, the fox played his role as surely as if he were traveling in packs like the wolf. He gained as much as he gave. The system made all foxes better hunters and more efficient scavengers, and it enhanced the natural scheme of the forest in two ways: disbursed food resources could be utilized, and solitary species could be maintained where highly social species might fail. A wolf pack would have been too much for the ecology of the conifer grove, while the services of the fox served well in the control of lesser animals. The fox, too, was served. The presence of other successful foxes meant a better chance to mate. The urine of the fox was but one more building block in the edifice of the natural forest system. If man finds an unlikely substance to be of great value, that is only because he has failed to learn the forest's first lesson. There are no unlikely natural substances.

And so the fox worked his way through the area as night fell, giving a silvery sheen to dark green needles and fallen logs. The decaying wood on which the mushrooms grew and on which the rest of the forest also fed was deceptive in its bulk. In 100 pounds of "dead" wood, gray by day but alive and metallic in moonlight, there was, should such a mass burn, but 1 pound of ash. The rest was water, carbon dioxide, and the sun's energy held tight for a while. Stored in the fibers of the wood, it all escaped as gas, either as the wood burned or as it slowly decomposed. What little was left, the ash from burning or the residue from slow decay, was all the more rich in minerals and chemicals drawn from both the earth and the sky. And that was what enriched the soil.

Ghost fingers and fronds of fern also reflected the ice light of the moon. Ferns are as characteristic as fungi in the moist forest. With alternating sexual and asexual generations, these ancient plants are well suited to the rich, shaded environment. Each year spores are produced on the graceful fronds in cases called sporangia, which, in turn, are grouped together in a sorus. By the shape of these sori one can determine the species of the fern. Each plant has two kinds of frond, one that is purely vegetative and the other fertile. When the spores mature, their cases turn dark brown and the sori look plump and fully round. When the sori burst and release their spores, each eager for life, the sori shrink and look depleted, as, in fact, they are.

Once free, the spores seek the hospitality of moist humus and soil, and in a few weeks hundreds of tiny, soft green plants called gametophytes form a velvet carpet. Each plant is heart-shaped with minute rhizoids anchoring it in place. These tiny plants are fragile and easily overlooked, but on each are the sex organs of the species, for this is that other kind of generation. The male organ, or antheridium, releases flagellated sperm which must literally swim to the female organ, or archegonium, attracted there by chemicals not unlike pheromones. Humidity near 100 percent is necessary for this sexual phase of the fern life cycle to begin. The biomass of fern plants in the moist forest is considerable, and its role in chemicals used, fixed, and contributed is, in turn, considerable. Among the most ancient plants, the ferns are playing the same role they played long before the first flowering plants were known on earth, or even the first birds. They come down from the time of the lizards and have adapted well, but unlike conifers and flowering plants, ferns have not freed themselves from a continual need of water. They are the amphibians of the plant world.

Dendragapus, the blue or sooty grouse, was a common visitor to the western hemlock stand. It was too damp for her species to nest there, but not much farther up the slope, where moisture was less likely to accumulate, she and many others of her kind had scratched nests into the ground in sheltered places and had laid eggs colored cinnamon to buff and marked with small, well-scattered chocolate spots. The grouse came to the hemlock and the Douglas fir to feed. Some insects were taken, some spiders and other invertebrates, but vegetable matter made up over 90 percent of her diet: berries, leaves, fruits, pine needles, all offerings of a coniferous forest with a healthy and varied understory. The forest was a table always set.

Among the most elusive of all the night animals of the hemlock forest was *Strix*, the spotted owl. *Strix* owl species are few in numbers, but occur on every inhabited continent except Australia. In the western United States they prefer the opportunities the hemlocks and Douglas firs offer. Strictly nocturnal and shy, they are seldom seen, but with their large eyes, sensitive ears, and powerful talons the medium-sized, light brown, spotted birds are a powerful element in the forest's population control mechanism. Nesting in tree cavities, in nests unadorned, they raise their two to four young (most often two). Usually quiet, silent while hunting, they are animals that rarely fall into the ken of man.

It had taken extensive modification of the basic bird idea to create the *Strix* owl. Being both hunter and nocturnal, he required highly refined senses of sight and hearing. The eyes of the owl were huge, far larger in proportion to the overall animal than the eyes of most other living things. Facing forward, they allowed binocular vision, and that aided in depth perception. As in all birds, the owl's eyes were surrounded by small bony plates, but in the owl these plates had become elongated, forming, in effect, a bony tube. The lenses were large, and their resolution powers enhanced, resolution always being a problem for a bird that must work in reduced light. Because owls have been given a rather narrow field of view (110 degrees, as compared to 180 degrees in man and 340 in homing pigeons), another accommodation had been necessary. The owl could rotate his head to a degree possible for few other animals. Other birds of prey can turn their heads 180 degrees. The *Strix* owl has a scanning movement of 270 degrees. All this meant that the owl could work effectively at between 1/10 and 1/100 the light intensity needed by man.

But sight was not enough. In the dark world of the forest, night owls had to hear as well as to see. Their ear openings were long, vertical slits nearly as deep as the head itself. The outer edges of the owl's characteristic facial disks bore stiff, short feathers. These rimmed the flaps of skin that lined the edges of the ear openings. By moving those flaps and those feathers, the owl scanned his world, bringing sound in from different quarters and sorting out useless sounds from those that conveyed the signals of either danger or prey. The broad head, so much broader in the owl than in other birds, provided the needed separation of the eyes and the ear openings. The result was a bird that could sit on a branch in almost total darkness and select its prey as it moved across the forest floor. With feathers softened for silent flight, the owl could drop from his branch and within seconds roll his powerful talons closed over a meal few other animals would have been able to detect. One of the most secretive members of the forest's storied community, *Strix* played his role every night amid the firs and hemlocks, generation after generation. Few of the lesser animals did not have an antecedent or descendant that had not become food for the silent spotted one of the night. Because animals beyond their prime become careless and noisy, hunters like *Strix* all but eliminate the possibility of old age in the forest.

Glaucomys sabrinus, the northern flying squirrel, had been born in a small tree hole 30 feet above the ground. Blind and pink, weighing 1/10 ounce, the tiny mote had been one of a litter of seven, born after a forty-day gestation period. It had grown quickly on its mother's milk, and before many months had passed, it had moved out of its hole to cling to the bark of the tree and wait for its time to sail into the night. The flying squirrel was also nocturnal. It could do little to protect itself from predators except flee, and to do that, it could not truly fly, only glide. By extending its legs, it could stretch a membrane that would buoy it up, but it could not flap or ascend. It had to glide down and climb up. It fed on mushrooms as well as on berries, seeds, and insects, so occasional trips were made to the hazardous forest floor.

On this night *Glaucomys* would seek the wine red *Helvella* mushrooms. They were ripe and ready along the rotting logs. By whatever means it can know such things and make decisions, the little gliding mammal decided on a trip involving the ultimate risk. Moving like a nervous little man on a darkened street, the squirrel popped halfway out of its hole and froze. It waited ten minutes, then emerged fully and moved a foot down the trunk. Again it waited almost ten minutes, frozen, listening. There were no sounds or threats, so the squirrel kicked loose. It dropped and broke its descent with an upward twist of the front half of its body, landing softly, almost completely silent, on a log where mushrooms grew in neat lines and small clusters. Again the squirrel froze for several minutes, before it felt safe to move to the first mushroom and begin to eat. It had been nearly a half hour since it first poked its head out of its tree hole. It saw nothing, heard nothing, until there was a slight nudge. It lasted only a fraction of a second. Then the squirrel was airborne again, but before its feet left the log, the spotted owl's talons had rolled shut.

Later that night another flying squirrel would begin to emerge from the same hole. Before its head was an inch clear of the opening, the owl's mate would pluck it

Before its head was an inch clear of the opening!

from its nest. Both owls fed well that night, and more flying squirrels would be born to replace those taken. The next day, when shafts of sun replaced the cold silver of night, the fox would come there again, and the grouse as well. The fox would take the grouse. The forest system worked around the clock, day and night.

11

Tsuga, the western hemlock, a tree that matures at two hundred and may well live past seven hundred years, is relatively disease-resistant, as its longevity attests. But while it is much hardier than most trees, there are still enemies in the forest that seek to bring it down. The 200-foot monarch in which the eagle perched on her second day in the forest had proved itself strong scores of times since its roots first curled down from the seed to seek sustenance in a nurse log. Multiple forces had conspired to test it at every stage of its growth and in its every part.

With luck the seed of the eagle's roost tree had found a deposit of rich, moist pulp. A following summer of drought, uncharacteristic of the region, had not harmed it. There were blights, too, growths with formidable names of tree hate—*Rhizina*, *Thelephora*, and *Phytoph-thora*—that twisted a seed, coated it, and made it rot. They had come, but this tree's seed had been strong enough. Others nearby had perished as some always must. This seed was destined to grow.

Once a tree has taken form and started its journey to the sky, the foliage, in this case blunt needles, is subjected to attack by corruption: rusts, molds, fungi that coat the needles in black, sooty secretions or turn them brown one at a time. The young hemlock had lost some needles and some branches, and in parts, at times, it had looked sick and ill-destined. But it had fought off the invaders, refused them purchase, and they had fallen away with the diseased needles and the sickened branches and become part of the floor debris. Later the tree would feed upon their dissolved chemicals as they seeped into the soil, their spread facilitated by worms.

The genus *Tsuga* is generally free of what the forest student calls stem diseases. Some cankers cause the tree to swell abnormally and secrete juices that leave small disfigurements, though few hemlocks die that way. In some stands, however, almost a third of the western hemlocks are parasitized by hemlock dwarf mistletoe, a killer known to science as *Arceuthobium*. It stunts the tree, retards its growth, and finally strangles it, falling to earth with its victim. This hemlock was born in an area where the dwarf mistletoe was less common, and it had not been set upon.

In areas of the trunk where dead bark formed and canker sores caused an excessive flow of resin, there had been colonization by fungi that caused disfigurement. But damage had been slight, barely more than cosmetic. Other fungi caused patches of black, sooty waste and ugly, brown, furlike mats, but in time they, too, perished and were shed. The tree survived all lower forms that attempted to bring it down.

There were only small scars to show the tests *Tsuga* had known. The history of the tree was written in rings within and scars without.

The roots of the Douglas fir had been tested, too. Drawing upon the power of the entire tree, the tangled mass had fought off an invasion of stringy yellow fungi pushing through the soil, a kind that will often rot the roots of northern conifers. There were other attempts to fell that fir—brown, mushy cushions of decay that followed the yellow streamers. The roots had pushed on, and the parasitic organisms had died off and fallen away.

A bear had come through the area when the Douglas fir was still young and sharpened its claws on the bark. These wounds wept and were invaded, and fungi grew. By the time the tree was a century old the scars were covered. There had been no rot of heartwood and no weakening of structure that could bring the tree down before a wind.

Twenty-one different fungi had attempted to overcome these two beneficent hosts, and all twenty-one had failed. The discolored mats and beards and growths had dwindled and shriveled and peeled off before the wind and the water that ran so often down the trunks of the giant plants. Other western hemlocks, Douglas firs, and red cedars nearby perished, but not these trees. From nodding crowns to probing root tips they had been assaulted every day of their lives by some life-form, singly or in combination. The trees denied them all. *Tsuga* and *Pseudotsuga*, the western hemlock and the Douglas fir, grew to earn the name of patriarch. They were giants and deserved to be.

The elk came and stood beneath the Douglas fir. He looked across to where the bear had locked his life for those brief moments with the snakes and rolled back his lip slightly. He knew the bear had been there, and although far fleeter than the shuffling, ambling hulk, the elk felt his own weakness. He could be surprised, dependent as he was on the shifting wind to announce the presence of danger. The bear might be slow most of the time, but he was also an explosive power. A bear not seen and not smelled because the wind blew from the wrong quarter could come forth from a brush pile or from behind a fallen log with such energy that even an elk could fall. And now the winds were tricky, left unsettled by yesterday's storm.

The elk was a male and bore antlers festooned with strips of velvet. The time had come when the velvet had to be stripped away. The tines of those antlers would have to be sharp and damaging, or at least intimidating, for the male was mature and would seek to claim females against the insistent claims of other males certain to come that way. Those antlers had their own story.

An antler and a horn are two very different things. Horns, like those of a cow, are permanent. They start growing while the animal is young and, unless lost to mischance, remain with the animal until it dies. If lost, they are not replaced. An antler, though, is a happening. It is grown each year and lost. The only exception recorded on earth is in the plains animal called pronghorn (mistakenly called antelope by many, although it is no more an antelope than a goat). The pronghorn alone of all animals on earth grows horns and sheds them.

In the spring of that same year the bull elk had shed his antlers; that had been in March, six months earlier. As the breeding season passed (and as the scent of the females ceased to stimulate the bull), he underwent hormonal changes. The bone at the pedicle, or base, of the antler began to erode, and one day as he brushed a tree, the left one came away. A few hours later, troubled by the new and disturbing imbalance, the bull jammed the other against a fallen log and broke it away as well. Blood oozed at the two sites, but scabs formed in normal course. In a few days the pedicles healed, and another antler cycle was completed.

Very shortly after the antlers came away to contribute quantities of calcium to the forest floor, the bull entered a period of explosive growth. His appetite began to increase. His intake of minerals grew steadily, for the events that were to follow needed all the support he could provide. If the elk's mineral intake fell below a certain required level, his antlers would still grow, but they would sap his entire body, would weaken him, and thereby could deny him his harem when the cold weather slipped down the slope again.

The new antlers that grew up from the recently healed pedicles were covered with hair and skin called velvet. Blood circulated through the velvet until shorter days signaled hormones within the bull and told his chemistry to shift. The circulation within the velvet stopped, and like a fabric, it began to tatter. It was then that it was stripped away by being rubbed and honed on rocks and trees or any other growth or structure near at hand and strong enough to take the prodding weight of the increasingly anxious bull.

In other areas with a poor supply of phosphorus, the elk's antlers would have been poor and perhaps misshapen. But at the edge of the forest, where there was varied undergrowth and around the perimeter of which there was good forage (and seepage from melting snow higher up the slope carrying other minerals to the areas of rich vegetational decay), this bull's antlers were forming well and would be commanding when the females ripened in the last weeks of fall and early winter.

The strings of velvet that were peeling away from the elk's splendid rack seemed to bother him. He shook his head often and ate the pieces that came free. The antlers showed bright pink where newly revealed. They would turn to brown with ivory tips. The elk would eat less as the days passed now, and move more alertly and with a more nervous step. He smelled for the bear again.

The name by which we know the elk is in itself confusing. It is properly *wapiti* and not *elk* at all. We have in more northern places an even larger deer (for the wapiti is a deer) called moose. But that word is used in North America alone. In the Scandinavian countries

and eastward into Siberia there are identical animals
—*Alces* is their universal name—but in all other places
our moose is called elk. Only by reverting to the name
wapiti for our elk and to *elk* for our moose could we
join the rest of the world in speaking of the largest deer.

The elk that stood near the Douglas fir worrying,
briefly, about the recent passage of the bear was a
giant. He was 100 inches long and stood 60 inches at the
shoulders. His neck was thick and ready to wield his
new antlers in terrible battle. He weighed just a few
pounds short of half a ton. Only the elk of the Old
World (or the moose of the New) could be a bigger deer
than this. He was at his heaviest now, for his compul-
sive eating to facilitate antler growth had added to his
bulk. He was prime and ready and would fight the
world to survive and to claim the females he needed to
stamp the future with his kind.

Already he was beginning to build a woolly undercoat against the winter that was still many weeks away.
He was characteristically brown and gray, each color
fading into the other on his broad flanks. There were
particularly rich shades of brown lower down, and a
tawny rump patch bordered in near black. His head
was brown, and lighter rings circled his alert and
searching eyes. A mane that would add to his look of
greater power was forming on his neck. He would not
only have to fight but intimidate.

The antlers that had grown throughout the summer
had a characteristic shape. There was a single long
beam that swept up and back from the skull, from the
pedicles on which they had grown. Each bore six tines

or points, and unlike the moose, there was no palmation, or flattened, platelike area.

The brow tines and the bay, or bez, tines were close to each other, very near the base of the whole fighting structure. They extended out above the muzzle and formed into four deadly points. The tray, or tres, tines arose farther up the beam. The smaller, or surroyal, tines appeared at the forking end of the main beam. The spread of the antlers passed 67 inches. The mighty wapiti seemed a fit opponent for any that would oppose his purpose of life or breeding.

The bear scent was still unmistakable, but now faint enough to be ignored. Yet there was another stronger scent, one the elk had learned well as a calf, for his mother had panicked several times when they had encountered it together. It came to him now, and again he rolled his lip. He tried to find it, but he wasn't certain. He knew only that it was close. He snorted, moved his tail a bit, and squealed *Eoughhhhh*, his alarm cry of all seasons, *Eoughhhhhhhh*.

12

 A few hundred yards from where the elk stood fast, a stream, fed continuously spring, summer, and fall by snow melting farther up the slope, bubbled up from below and soaked the ground before forming again into a discrete surface channel. From a spruce overhead came a torrent of sound.

In the strangely musical language of the Chinook Indians he was *ap-poe-poe*. To early European settlers he was the chickaree or sometimes the piney sprite. To John Muir this forest elf was "without exception, the wildest animal I ever saw—a fiery, sputtering little bolt of life."

Tamiasciurus douglasii, the Douglas squirrel, was the bigmouth of the fir and hemlock forest. Never content with his own affairs, he variously whistled, chirped,

and sang his frenetic way through each day. The bear
that had ended the life of the king snake had passed
beneath his perch the day before and had been met
with foot stamping and tail flicking. Now a woodpecker's tapping on an adjacent Douglas fir was answered
by a swirling motion that carried the sprite around the
trunk of his tree three times in rapid succession with no
purpose other than to participate.

He was a pretty animal, though not a large one. Five
inches of his 14-inch length consisted of flat, bushy tail.
His upper parts ranged from olive to dark brownish
gray or grayish brown, depending on the light in which
he was seen. Along each side was a narrow black band
separating the darker upper part from the lower, which
itself varied from yellowish white to bright orange. His
tail was fringed gaily with white-tipped hairs. Slight
tufts grew on the sprite's ears. In the winter the tufts
would turn black and brown.

This bolting flash of color tumbling through the conifers' upper stories was a benefactor of the forest. He ate
pine seeds, handling some cones that weighed as much
as 5 pounds. He shredded the cones, throwing aside
the scales and digging for the fine seeds deep inside.
The larger cones, cut loose by the sprite's extremely
sharp teeth, thumped to earth, and after ascertaining
that the area was free of predators, he descended after
them. Owls, hawks, eagles, weasels, coyotes, wolves,
bobcats, mountain lions—all were his enemies, although he could find safety from most when tucked in
tight against a tree trunk high above the ground or in
flight to thin branches that would hold him alone.

The Douglas squirrel was not a neat or economical feeder. He wasted much, but his waste was the forest's gain. Many earlier hidden cones were forgotten or lost, but since he was programmed to store his hoardings near streams or at least in moist soil, where cones are best preserved, much of those lost hoardings germinated. A good percentage of the trees that grew in the conifer forest had been sown in the gardens of the sprite.

He had far too much to say, but somehow he was more amusing than troublesome in his usually unnecessary comments, his inconsequential challenges. Together with his movements, caught in shafts of light and set against shifting greens, browns, and grays, they were an essential part of the forest—perhaps, in some strange way, its comic relief and excitement.

There were some members of the sprite's forest audience that saw him as more than mere amusement, that watched and waited for those moments when he would be so full of himself, so excited by his own excellence of noise and being, he would forget that single most critical of all lessons: the fact that his flesh was sweet and good when full of cones, mushrooms, and the seeds of trees. His teeth were strong and sharp, but he was easily grasped where they could do no good, could not be brought into play. His only real defense was a combination of alertness and speed, in equal quantities. Without either, for only a second in times of danger, his life would end, and his tree fall silent.

On this day, however, the obstreperous sprite had the wit to recall that lesson. In the midst of his aerial gyrations he had spotted a cluster of mushrooms on the forest floor. A quick descent and he was there, nibbling on the fungus. Suddenly, by signals unknown to us, he was aware of a pair of eyes—dark, intense, hungry— watching him through a screen of pale green ferns at the edge of the forest glade. His recognition of those eyes turned him from carefree sprite into fearful prey. Instantly he was back in the tree. But for this danger the gap between ground and tree branch would not be enough. Once aloft, the squirrel leaped from his spruce to a higher branch on the Douglas fir next to it, then on from one tree to the next, sailing across gap after gap until he had covered a half mile. Exhausted, he spread himself on a thick branch, allowing his legs to dangle while he slept.

The female pine marten, *Martes americana*, also lived near the stream. She weighed just over 5 pounds and was 26 inches long. A third of her length was well-furred, bushy tail. Her upper body was a warm, lustrous brown with shiny guard hairs and a thick, luxuriously soft undercoat. Her underside was light orange, close to the color of the squirrel's belly. Her throat was distinctively yellow-white, while her legs, paws, ears, and tail were almost black. She was a beautiful animal and an efficient hunter, like all the weasel kind.

The previous July, on a warm and humid night, she had met a mate. She had come across a streak of scent he had rubbed along a high branch from a gland in the region of his stomach. She had followed the scent for a quarter of a mile, leaping from tree to tree, picking it up at or near each landing site. She made a chuckling sound as she moved, and in time the male appeared. They had a total of fifteen days for their breeding season and had to mate during that period. They did so, several times, and then they parted. There had been a characteristic delayed implantation of the embryos, and it wasn't until 236 days later that four pale yellow, fuzzy young were born in a moss-lined nest within a hollow tree. The marten had carefully prepared the site as the time approached. Her young were blind and helpless at first, and she had had to nurse them for six weeks before forcing them onto solid food. Even then she had had to hunt with extra determination, for they were as dependent on her for food after they were weaned as they had been before.

The marten will take a variety of prey—rabbits, ground-nesting birds, other weasels, even some vegetable matter—but the marten's favorite food is plump squirrel.

There is a reason why the marten's choicest prey should be a tree animal. The marten is one of the Mustelidae, the family to which all weasels belong, and weasels in general, because they are so competitive and aggressive, have developed specialized methods of hunting. The otter has no mammalian peer in fresh water, and the feisty, testy badger burrows faster, deeper, and farther than any of the other Mustelidae. The marten can compete with neither of these cousins, which will also hunt on land if that is where the food is. But so will the coyote, the bobcat and lynx, and the mountain lion. The land is a wild and dangerous arena for predators, which will take prey not only from other predators but also each other. The marten, with its extraordinary speed, excels high above the ground. There no competitor can touch it. The marten is to the upper layers of the forest what the eagle is to the sky. It can and at times does hunt below, but it is at its best and most secure aloft.

The marten (sometimes confused with the sable, its Russian cousin) does not appear to be specially adapted for life in the treetops. True, its body is elongated, as is the case with most weasels, the luxuriant tail probably does offer some balance and rudder effect during athletic leaps and spirals in the upper stories, and the furred pads of its feet may provide added traction when landings are attempted in thin, swaying branches. But it is apparently its musculature that gives the marten the precision and sense of balance that make it the swiftest mammal in the Western Hemisphere above the ground. Only monkeys can rival the marten aloft, and they dwell in a different kind of forest in a different climate.

The female pine marten had been feeding on a ground squirrel, *Citellus*, taken where the stream entered the forest growth, when she had spotted the more desirable Douglas squirrel come to earth to feed on mushrooms. As the sprite frantically ascended the spruce, the marten made no move. She knew what she could do. There was time.

She had consumed only a portion of the ground squirrel. Now she scraped some grass and leaves over the rest of the carcass. She moved carefully around the tangle of ferns into the forest again and across the open space to where the squirrel had been feeding. She started up the spruce, careening off branches and trunk with the ease of the wind, climbing higher and higher as if the very tree had been designed for her ease and convenience. She was soon at a point high enough for her to know that her prey had moved away. Then she, too, settled down and rested on a branch close to the trunk. Her colors blended into the lights and shadows of that second forest world, high above the forest floor, so that she nearly vanished. Seventy feet below and off beyond the ferns, a coyote found the remains of the ground squirrel and, pawing away the debris, dragged the treasure off to eat at its convenience.

It was still morning, and the marten was in no hurry. The squirrel could be followed—traced by the marten's incredible sensitivity to the sprite's odor—and afternoon was a more pleasant time to hunt. A half mile apart, the two adversaries dozed.

By two o'clock the pine marten decided to hunt. Having eaten very little of the ground squirrel, she was feeling hunger again. Experience had taught her that despite her small ritualistic efforts at covering her prey, it would not be there if she bothered to return. The sprite, so full of pine seeds and himself, could solve her problems for the rest of the day and night. It was a simple equation, and a familiar one: death times one equals life for another, and sometimes many.

At two-fifteen the marten finished her second circuit of the spruce. She moved to the topmost branches, and although they swayed in a way that might seem precarious to us, she was in no danger. As the tip bent

He ran onto the finest branches before leaping to other trees — tireless

over, she dropped free and landed on the lower branch of the adjoining fir, running even as she landed. She descended the tree, then climbed up another nearby. She accomplished this by quickly, powerfully striking the trunk downward with her forefeet, then careening off and spiraling upward. She was liquid agility itself. No other mammal could match the ease with which she canvassed the trees, searching into the highest perches. She darted her head in and out of holes and crevices;

in fluidity and speed — The marten was no less so in her pursuit.

she sniffed along branches; she leaped from tree to tree. Aside from the hum of branches whipping back into place after she had passed and the whisper of the foliage against her silken body, there were no sounds. Silent, solitary, she moved like the sighing wind and sought the death of the squirrel.

The squirrel, in fact, sensed her approach, as he had sensed her stare on the forest floor, and being unable to control his urgent need to provide commentary, he whistled, scolded, chortled, and was off. The first hint of sound from the piney sprite triggered the marten into full hunting mode. The two animals, both masters of the chase in high places, ripped through the treetops like silken arrows of brown and orange light. The squirrel started 70 feet ahead of the marten but could not hold his lead. He practiced every evasive tactic his own evolutionary development had taught him. He rappelled off trunks, but so did the marten. He swirled around to the far side of heavy boles and branch junctures, but the marten was there seconds later. He ran out onto the finest branches before leaping to other trees, but the marten did the same, though always jumping a little sooner to avoid the possible breaking of a branch. Thus she had to leap a bit farther, but still she stayed close behind.

The squirrel seemed tireless in the fluidity and speed of his flight. The marten was no less so in her pursuit. In time the squirrel would err. The marten would be there, and it would end.

The squirrel's flight took him to the edge of the growth. He was unwilling to drop to the ground, and the nearest tree, beyond the clearing, was 60 feet away. That was too great a leap. He swerved to reenter the thickest part of the grove in the vain hope of losing the marten there, leaped, and landed on a firm branch. The marten was there first. Sharp killing teeth clasped, were repositioned, then broke through the squirrel's spine where it emerged from its skull. It was so quick there was no more than a shiver and probably little pain. In seconds the piney sprite's body hung across the branch, and the marten, panting, stood with both front paws resting on her kill. She had won again. It was why she had chosen to hunt aloft. On the ground she was as good as many, a little better than some, and a little worse than others. But up here, at the level where the eagle sat, where trees like hemlocks and firs touch the winds above the earth, the marten was queen and her sometime mate king. Other piney sprites would sass and argue and whistle and scold. But this one would not, not ever again. A small quantity of noise and color was gone from the world.

The mate of the California ground squirrel which the marten had taken earlier, and then had abandoned for the coyote to find, died that day as well. *Otospermophilus beecheyi*, 11 inches of brown and buffy white, he bore a conspicuous dark triangle between his shoulders. His tail was somewhat bushy, but generally less so than that of his more aerially inclined cousins the tree squirrels. His natural habitat was pastures and grainfields, and he did not like thick chaparral in drier country or the dense forest of this moister slope. He would come down the slope, though, close to where the trees stood tall and where ferns and bushes marked the higher forest boundary. It was in such a place that his mate had died that day when the marten shot off a tree and exploded through the barrier of ferns. Now he, too, in fatal carelessness, exposed himself—to the sun, and to the eyes of the eagle. Hardly caring about the wapiti's apprehension of danger in the growth under the adjoining Douglas fir, *Aquila* saw the squirrel easily—she could have seen a mouse at fifty times the distance—and dropped away on a slow-rising thermal. The ground squirrel barely saw her shadow. Before his first muscle could contract to give him enough spurt and speed to escape, the talons of the golden hunter closed, and his spine was in shreds. For a moment the bird rose into the air to hover over her kill, shrouding the squirrel with her extended wings to satisfy herself, in the fashion of eagles, that there were no challengers. Then she landed back on him, pulled him apart easily, and fed. It was over in minutes, for he was small prey for so large a bird. Once finished, she hopped and ran easily into the wind, then soared over the forest twice before dropping back onto her branch. The ground squirrel had been an hors d'oeuvre, and soon there would be more substantial fare to draw her off her branch again.

13

The western hemlock and its associated trees stood upslope within the compass of a ring 20 miles in diameter. At the downslope limit of the forest, far from the eagle's perch, stood an area of dense growth that was the established hunting ground of *Martes pennanti*, the fisher. Once more common and more widespread than it is now, *Martes* had always been what scientists call a culture fleer. It avoids the proximity of man, for where dense forest growth is cut away, the fisher is denied the habitat it must have to survive. It is a finely tuned natural mechanism, and its demands must be met or it vanishes.

People in their time have called the fisher many

names: pekan, black fox, fisher-marten, Pennant's cat, black cat. But those names misrepresent and mislead.

Martes is not a fox or a cat, but a weasel like the marten. When Europeans arrived in the New World, the fisher was one of the first treasures they identified. *Martes*'s fur was rich and could bring a high price from people who wore such things. The commercial pelt of the fisher was unique among weasel furs in that the female's proved more valuable than the male's, although the female might be little more than half the size of the male.

One of the largest of the mustelids, *Martes* when fully grown weighs 20 pounds and is 40 inches long. A foot of that length is luxurious, bushy tail. It is supple, short-legged, and has small, rounded ears. It also has the sharp sloping muzzle of a deadly hunter over eyes that are small, intense, keen, and very dark, as is its soul.

The fisher that owned this hunting range and guarded it with fury was a large male. Colors in his kind run from grayish dark brown to almost black, and this *Martes* appeared to be black, or nearly so. Glossy white-tipped guard hairs shone over much of his coat. His face, neck, and shoulders glistened with a silvery sheen as he moved from sunny areas into progressively darker shadows. He seemed to ripple as he moved, a powerful coil, all slow grace one moment and violent energy the next.

Like all the weasels, he had to hunt to survive. He could eat berries and nuts, but only in small quantities, and perhaps more as a relish than a staple food. He willingly ate carrion from kills he had made earlier or that had been left by others, but most of what he ate he had just killed—there and then, as needed. Despite his name, *Martes*, the fisher, took fewer fish in a year than most other weasels. Unless he came upon a salmon stream and found a ready supply of dead and dying fish, he took no fish at all. Although a strong swimmer, he did not willingly take to water unless it was necessary to avoid detection or to make a kill. But he hunted all other things that lived in the forest that were not too large for him to handle. Early white men who traveled with Indian bands said that a fisher would kill a deer, but such stories are almost certainly not true. Animals like *Martes* inspire legends, for they are rarely seen alive, and then only half-seen. They are a half-truth, then—of the eye of the mind.

No man had ever seen this fisher. He was too alert, too swift and agile. In fact, no prey animal that lived in his hunting range could outrun him or dodge effectively enough to long avoid his jaws. Rabbits, squirrels, other weasels, ground-nesting birds, porcupines when he could find them—all fell easily to this magnificent assassin of the shadowed forest. He could go aloft, like the marten, but he spent most of his time on the ground or streaking along fallen logs. Wherever trees grew in his forest, around their base or on lower trunks and boughs, this weasel was a savage nemesis to his prey.

The fisher led a largely solitary life. He had always lived and hunted alone, except for regular April encounters that had begun in his second year. Each year since, when spring finally broke winter's grip, the male had listened for the enticing *churrs* and *chuckles* of a female. His encounters were not prolonged, and the female would immediately make off and wait fifty weeks before her cubs would be born in a natural cavity of rock or in a fallen log. (As it is with many weasels, the implantation of the embryo is delayed in the fisher, and the gestation period is made to appear unnaturally long.) Except for his part in those encounters, the male fisher was alone for all the year. His hunting territory was marked and belonged to him alone. With skunk-like glands he declared his sovereignty. He would fight most terribly with any other of his kind that dared intrude.

The fisher's senses were keen. Ears, eyes, nose—all played a role in determining a profitable targeting direction. From a blind, hairless kit lying helpless on a dark bed of beaten grass, destined to nurse for seven weeks before first tasting solid food, had grown a killer without peer.

Lepus americanus, the snowshoe hare, was shy. His kind was hunted by virtually every predator that stalked his range. In fact, no hare dies of old age. All grow old and careless; all are taken. Hares are often referred to as rodents, but that is clearly an error. Rabbits, jackrabbits, and hares are lagomorphs, and there are distinctions enough in skull structure to satisfy the scientists who must deal with such facts. There is confusion, too, between rabbits and hares. One clear distinction is that rabbits are born helpless and pink, while hares and jackrabbits are born fully furred and far advanced. Hares and jackrabbits, too, are generally larger than their rabbit kin and have longer ears and more powerful hind legs.

The snowshoe hare had an easy, bouncy gait. Five- or 10-foot leaps were well within his ability, as were quick midair twists and changes of direction. Capable of lying still for hours, the snowshoe could explode and appear to rebound off invisible walls midair as he fought to live another day. That morning the snowshoe had hunkered down under a rusty leaf bush. Now he sensed the presence of the fisher. Of all the animals from which *Lepus* had cause to flee, the fisher was one of the most dangerous.

Before *Lepus* and *Martes* could react to each other, there was a disturbance in the area. Strangers had come to the forest, foreign beings of ill-defined type and disposition. The fisher sensed their unbalancing presence immediately and went aloft. He floated up the trunk of a smaller Douglas fir as easily as he could have flowed along a log. He would wait and see. He was hungry, as usual, but he could wait.

The five strangers that moved into the forest that day were exotics—foreign canines whose kind is now insinuating itself into the wildlife makeup of this continent. They are a fine idea gone bad, the distortion of what began as a brilliant stroke of socially evolving man.

Every naturally occurring wild animal is fixed to its own genetic potential. Each creature of the forest is and always has been a point in time, a place along the way

The five strangers that moved into the forest.

in evolutionary development. The fisher, for example, has certain potential as an individual animal. Every experience it has, every encounter in its life challenges it, but it has only its own stuff upon which to draw. If the fisher is not fast enough, it loses the race. If it loses too many races, it dies as an individual. And if all its kind follow suit, then its species dies as well. Each truly wild animal is stuck with this demand to adapt—either to win or to fail and die. For the fisher, as well as the marten, the fox, the rattlesnake, grouse, or eagle, there is no new pool of genetic material, and what may lie ahead for them is determined strictly by what has gone before. In the context of the cosmos each such creature is an arrow of life shot forward through time.

The wild creatures that came up the valley slope, their snouts and teeth working like scythes, were not tied to such a well-defined potential, for they had been helped all along the way by man—first helped and then abandoned.

Perhaps twenty thousand years ago men living in caves took in the pups of wolves and jackals. They were toys for the young, we think, then camp followers that became fixed to nomadic human bands. Somehow— and all we can do is speculate about the details—man and canids joined. By ten thousand years ago the people of Sumeria had taken that idea and produced what was probably the world's first purebred dog. That dog is known today as the Saluki.

And so it has been for at least one hundred centuries. Man has styled these animals, has made them what he wanted them to be. Still all of one species, they are as variable as the Great Dane and the Chihuahua, the Poodle and the Bloodhound. And it is all that breeding to special style that stood behind the feral dogs that came to the forest that day.

Man is not careful with his treasures. He has always wasted, has always thrown away as much or more than he has kept. And so it has been with his dogs. Wherever he has gone man has taken his dogs, has lost them and abandoned them. Around the world these animals, ten millennia out of the wild, have been required to reseek their own living, as pariahs both near man and in the wild.

But once returned to the wild, once feral, dogs have an advantage over all other wildlife, an advantage based on the special things man originally bred them for. Although the fisher can draw on no new potential, the dog can. If a dog pack in the wild is too slow, it need only wait. Sooner or later a faster dog—a Greyhound, perhaps, or some other fleet breed—will join it, and the puppies produced will be faster. If a pack of free-living dogs has poorer eyesight than would best facilitate its survival, it need only wait for a sight hound to join it, and the same would be true for a pack's ability to smell, for there are always Bloodhounds, Beagles, Coonhounds, Harriers, and Foxhounds. All that potential created by man from the amazingly elastic species he first domesticated is always there, to flow in and increase the wild dog's advantage over native wildlife. The scale tips farther each year.

In the five dogs that came that day to the lower limit of the fir and hemlock forest could be recognized the genius of the German breeder Ludwig Dobermann, who at the end of the nineteenth century developed a pinscher to suit his taste. The sleek efficiency and sharp senses of the Doberman Pinscher served the pack well.

When the Roman legions invaded Asia, they captured animals that had been bred there since before the first records of history. We do not know this dog well, but we refer to it as the Molossian type. The Romans fostered this breed and made it fiercer still. It fought for them in the arenas and then crossed with the legions over the Alps as guards of the camp and herders of cattle. That Molossian type became the ancestral stock of the Saint Bernard and the Bernese Mountain Dog. That ancient Molossian blood from Asia via Rome and Switzerland was in the band, too, and it was another source of strength.

A thousand years ago, in Spain, a dog of Spain or "spanielle" evolved. Examples of these fast, smart dogs were taken to other parts of the European continent and to England. They were bred up and down into lines we today call setter and spaniel. The five-dog pack was smarter and keener in the hunt because one of its members shared the blood of the ancient dogs of Spain.

The ancient Hungarians, on the harsh steppes where they made their home, bred a dog remembered as the Aftscharka, a dog with blood that probably ran back in more ancient times to Tibet. When the Huns invaded from the East, they moved through, stealing dogs as they went. Descended from these dogs are the Komondor and perhaps the Puli. That blood was also there that day in the forest.

In Turkish there is a word, *kawasz*, which means "he

who would protect nobility with arms." It is also the name of a dog, the Kuvasz, and that blood ran with the pack and unbalanced the forest system this day.

The farmers who lived in the highlands where England and Scotland meet developed breeds of dogs that would work for them in sport and industry. They needed ratters and fighters, animals that could be counted on and bet on as well. Many strains of fighting ratters emerged, and the best of them have survived into our time. We call them terriers. They are sharp, hot little dogs, and their heritage added fire to the pack and made it a keener group of dogs as they moved into the forest.

Almost two thousand years ago the Romans conquered Württemberg in the country we know today as Germany. In the seesaw of battle some of the Roman dogs that had come as companions and fellow soldiers were lost. Later the Germans bred those dogs of Rome. Especially in the city of Rottweil on the Neckar River southwest of Stuttgart was the massive-jawed breed fostered. Butchers used them to herd their cows to market, and then, when it came time to return home with the proceeds of the sale, these men would tie their bags of money to the necks of their dogs. No thief would seek it there, not if he valued his life. The Rottweiler history ran with the pack, and although the butchers who drove their cows along the muddy paths of Germany meant nothing to the forest, the strength they had bred into their dogs was about to tell.

It was the history of man, then, a history built into the companion dog, that slipped in through the brush along the forest's edge—the red bilberry, the Oregon grape, the creambush, and the stink currant—early that afternoon. Having spent the night scattered .over a grassy vale, each curled into a ball, each no closer to another than 3½ or 4 feet, the dogs had slept. With first light they were up, stretching and urinating, and then they had come together. There had been some socializing, nibbling of muzzles, some whining, and a small show of dominance as a younger dog appeared too bold and began sniffing the rear of a bitch now four days beyond her heat. One of the larger dogs bared his teeth and snarled, and the lesser animal rolled over, twisted his neck to expose the carotid artery, and whined. The dominant dog pressed his bared teeth against the proffered throat and rumbled his prior right, deep in his well-ribbed chest. The lesser dog whined again, and it was enough; the larger dog moved away, and the smaller rolled upright and ran behind the other, mock nipping at his feet. Dogs, like wolves, do not have to fight. Submission by one arrests the other and holds him to a gentler course. The ritual is fixed, dictated by social needs. Feral though they were, these dogs had not forgotten the wild etiquette they had carried with them into the first cave when they began to share their life with man. Perhaps in the wild again it was, in fact, reemerging, unlocking traits and skills sequestered during the centuries of domestication.

There was no dog in the pack that was more than three generations removed from the hearth. Two of the dogs had grown up in the company of man. One, a Labrador-Collie mix, had been cast away when its family moved and decided they didn't want the bother of an old animal in a new neighborhood. They could always adopt another from the pound, they justified, and one afternoon they opened the car door and pushed their bewildered friend out "to fend for himself." The other recent companion of man, a Doberman-Rottweiler cross, had wandered off from a commercial campsite, and by the time he had found his way back his master's camper bus was gone. Always suspicious of strangers, the large, short-haired dog had not lent himself to adoption. Looking dangerous and acting shy and nervous, he had been driven off every time he approached human beings. He had been stoned and once even shot at. After finding the pack, he had easily become its dominant member.

The three other dogs represented, in varying degrees, the other breeds we have spoken of. In small part or large they carried that blood and that history, and now, leaving the grassy slope, they sought the forest just above them and their meal. Packs of dogs are always hungry and will always kill. Unlike cats, they are not equipped to make that kill fast, smooth, and clean. They tear apart whatever they can find. And mouthfuls of meat may be swallowed before the victim is dead. This unappealing design was not the dog's idea.

It did not take the dogs long to find a small pile of carrion left by another hunter several days before. What had been a beautiful blue grouse now lay as bones and feathers and very little meat. The dogs ripped the scraps apart and moved on. One of the smallest members of the pack found a dead garter snake and rolled on it and was joined by two others. The snake was not eaten, yet the dogs would stink of it for days. [The smell pleased them.]

In their casting back and forth the dogs sensed the hare but could not find it. They pushed through every bush and snuffled around the base of every tree. The open ends of fallen logs were investigated, and few of them failed to provide some stimulation to the hunt, for each log had been used by some animal not once but many times, not by a single species but by several. The recent history of the forest was written in scent particles, and each chapter was followed by the dogs until it ran out. To animals with keen noses like dogs carrying scent-hound blood, such an area is a whole world invisible to man. We are like blind men in a museum. We can only be told what is there to behold.

Finally, a terrier type of dog, the second smallest member of the pack, flushed the hare. With its powerful hind legs and heavy feet, the hare sprinted, leaped, and twisted as the pack fell in behind, yelping and barking. Twice the hare was knocked to earth by dogs that almost but not quite got their jaws around him, but each time the frantic energy of the hare broke him loose. Each time he emerged unbloodied. The outcome of five hungry dogs against one hare is usually foretold, but now there was to be a different ending. One of his incredible bounding, twisting escape maneuvers landed the hare near the open end of a cavern formed by several heavy tree trunks that had long ago fallen to earth. With all five dogs only inches behind, he dived headlong into what could be his salvation or his deathtrap. As it happened, the tunnel between the trunks narrowed sharply, and the hare plunged on ahead, squeezing through a constriction to a broader space beyond.

Terriers were bred by man to go to ground, to follow vermin into their lairs, and to kill them there or drive them out into the jaws of hounds. Without hesitation the terrier-type member of the pack dived into the tunnel, too, followed by another, smaller dog. They wedged against each other and struggled until the terrier squeezed ahead. Digging frantically into the decaying wood, the little dog tried to follow the hare into the heart of the dead tree cave. While the other dogs raced up and down the length of the logs, whining and yapping in excitement, the terrier struggled to rip the heart out of the wood. It was not to be. The hare did not come out the far end, there were no other holes into the log den big enough for a dog to work at, and eventually the terrier had to back out and sit panting near the opening where the hare had vanished. The dog's feet were bloodied from his frantic digging.

The log jumble where the hare had found his haven lay not more than 10 feet from the tree where the fisher had gone aloft at the first sign of the dog pack. The fisher hung head down along the trunk, snarling in rage and pounding an abrupt tattoo against the tree with his forefeet. Other creatures, too, watched and worried, each in its own peculiar way. Packs of hunting dogs do not go unmonitored in the forest.

Had he dropped to earth, the fisher could probably have held his own against any single dog in the pack with the possible exception of the Alpha dog, the Doberman-Rottweiler cross. And even then there would have been some question of the outcome. But the pack was too much. Even the monumental rage of a giant weasel will not propel it willingly into the fury of five other sets of jaws.

The dogs flung their bodies against the tree, baying and yowling and leaping in an effort to get the sleek hunter that hung above their heads humming with rage, churring like a giant transformer on a high utility pole. A safe 12 feet separated the fisher from the strongest dog's highest leap. Soon the leaps became less frantic and less frequent, dwindling from half-hearted to nothing more than forepaws resting against the tree.

It was behavior wolves would not have succumbed to. Wolves would have waited near the tree and watched for the fisher to make the first move. Dogs, even longtime feral dogs, are still far removed from the calm intelligence of the true wolf. Dogs become hysterical; wolves do not.

When the dogs finally settled down, the fisher stopped his snarling and waited. When the dogs appeared to lose all interest, the fisher turned and ran farther up the trunk. He crossed from there to another tree, and then to another, and in seconds was gone. No dog could follow that trail, not even with the skill man had bred into his companions from the days of the cave.

The forest was in an extraordinary state of unrest from the coming of the dog pack. Noisier than any other animals and less precise in their behavior, in their coming and going, the dogs were not easily tolerated by the natural system. When they left the wood by early evening, they had still made no major kills and had done little damage. But animals like the fisher had done little hunting in that time, too. Almost in disgust each animal had withdrawn into the tightest compass of its world to wait for the noise and upheaval to pass. Such unrest is not the way it is done in the natural world, only among the cast-off animals of man.

As for the pack, it would shrink, then grow again as other straying and abandoned dogs joined it over the years. Some members would die on the highway, some would be shot by farmers and hunters, and some would die in traps. Disease would take some. But new blood would flow in, and crosses would occur with coyotes, perhaps even with wolves. In the throwaway dogs of America there may lie a terrible new predator, impossible competition for native wildlife. No one knows where the feral dog is going, but it is now a fixed and growing part of the American wildlife scene.

And the fisher, had he really been there at all? A forest ghost, diurnal one day, nocturnal the next, the fisher is one of those animals that slips through barriers of consciousness, back and forth, like a breeze that barely brushes the leaves. But there was a trail, evidence of the fisher's passing. A marten would hunt that tree in search of a squirrel and find it. Along the branch and on the trunk there would be a musky smell. Even a man pressing his nose to the bark would be able to sense it, although he might not know it from natural decay or mildew. But to all the other creatures who play aloft it was there, a warning smell. For unlike other ghosts we know, the fisher can come alive and explode full-fanged upon its neighbors. And the only proof, very often, that it exists at all is that scent, for it alone lingers when the leaves come to rest and the branches cease to move.

14

The cat ranged far in the course of his hunting life. He might cover 25 miles in a single day; a cryptic cat, he slipped from secret place to secret place, a hider and stalker and careful watcher of all that came within his sphere. Many cougars barely pass 100 pounds, even in their full maturity, but others, like the one that worried the wapiti that day in the hemlock-Douglas fir wood, was more than twice that size, almost 210 pounds of muscle and sinew and killing purpose.

The cougar is the second largest cat in the entire Western Hemisphere, smaller only than the spotted and rosetted jaguar. The tawny unmarked cougar has the greatest north-south range of any cat in the world.

From Argentina to Canada it stalks in its solitary way. Red golden to sand in color, it is beauty and power and secrecy.

A cougar is one of the greatest of all natural killing machines. Unlike dogs and packs of wolves, this cat does not wear or rip its prey down to die from exhaustion and shock. A cougar pounces and kills quickly. A neck is broken, a throat hard clamped to stop all flow of air. The reserve power a cat retains for the moment of killing is enormous.

A cougar is not a precocious species. The young are helpless when born in a cave or hollow log and are fed and nurtured and trained by a mother that will defend her young against all enemies. It is at their mother's side that the young cats play and are reprimanded and learn. One of the lessons learned is that the great wapiti does not surrender life easily. Most such giant deer taken by cougars are young or female, but even a large and antlered bull may be taken on occasion by a large and hungry cat.

The cougar hung back, shifting silently to avoid the focus of the wapiti's attention. At one point the cat went up the far side of a tree, a spruce, and came to rest 40 feet above the ground, with the elk testing the wind 100 yards away. The bull knew there was trouble but not yet where it lurked. It knew that it was a cat and was hunting. The wapiti sensed itself to be the intended prey. The smell of danger was clear.

Eoughhhhh, the bull squealed again. No other wapiti were near enough to hear him; it was merely a nervous release of sound. The cat heard it and shifted his position on the branch. Twice he started down the trunk, but both times he held a moment, then climbed back up again. The smell of the wapiti was strong, for the bull was releasing musk in nervous reaction to his growing awareness of cat presence. Each animal was working himself up; combat seemed inevitable. The cat was hungry, and the very size of the bull standing off in the gloom of the heavily shaded forest floor was taunting and threatening. The cougar could die casting such a challenge, but he could eat well, too, for many days. The carrion of a wapiti kill would be as welcome as the fresh muscle meat and offal. The cat was not so much a meat eater as an animal eater, and if he could take the wapiti, he would open its gut and eat the vegetable matter there; he would eat bone and sinew and hide and fur and even gnaw on velveted antlers and on hooves. The vast collection of minerals and fats and protein acids that constitute a living member of the deer family could build the great cat into a greater one still.

The cat watched from the tree, and the wapiti worried and moved, nervously seeking the cause of his concern. He could find his foe only in particles of scent, and even these were too spread out, too thin and without direction. They were just the barest hints of the danger that blanketed the park beneath the trees.

The wapiti could tolerate just so much pressure and then had to give, just as all animals must. His patience was less than that of a mature cat. The wapiti made the first move. He circled the Douglas fir twice, lifting his feet high in prancing nervousness, then moved toward the hemlock where the eagle had just returned from her ground squirrel kill. The eagle had been watching, but there was no game here for one of her size. She leaned forward now and glowered down. It was all an insult to her privacy and peace.

The wapiti did not stay long beneath the hemlock but moved off again, this time directly toward the tree where the cougar waited. What had been assumed as a sighting vantage point had become a platform for attack. The cat would not have to come to earth and stalk. The attack could now come from above.

Instinctively the cat knew the wapiti's antlers could end his life. If the great deer sensed the streaking death from above, he could twist his head in time, and the cat would find an array of tines waiting for his impact. He could be impaled, and although the crash of the cat might snap the wapiti's neck, the cat would die as well, twisting upon points now almost freed of velvet, sharp and ready for cat and other foes.

Still the wapiti did not locate the cat, perhaps because the cat was too high up or perhaps because the elk had never been attacked from above. He moved closer to the spruce. The cat crouched lower onto his branch and dug his claws deeper into the bark. Small twitching movements of his rear quarters betrayed the tension he felt and perhaps secured a final purchase. The wapiti moved closer, still rolling his lip and snorting and squealing, though softly now, *Eoughhhh*. Giant that he was, well armed for battle, the wapiti did not feel fear. It was rage that welled up. But one is as weakening as the other.

The cat crouched lower onto his branch — The wapiti

When the wapiti finally caught the full scent of the cat, it was too late to matter. More than 200 pounds of cougar were streaking down, forefeet out, from 42 feet above the ground. After 37 feet of free fall they struck the wapiti on the withers at 23½ miles per hour and took him to earth. Before the antlers could be hooked, the cat had moved to a catching place in his prey's twisting body. His hind feet raked across the rib cage; his foreclaws reached the nose pad of the struggling

140

wapiti. The great deer expelled air rapidly and tried to squeal and then to shake his head, but even his mighty neck muscles could not dislodge the cat, not with his head arched back. The sound of the bull's neck breaking was muffled by the sound of both animals thrashing on the forest floor. The wapiti was not yet dead, but he was paralyzed. The numbness crept down through his body as the brain was disconnected from all of him that could resist what was about to happen. The cat

moved closer, still rolling his lip – snorting and squealing.

shifted and clamped his jaws on the wapiti's throat. The air flow stopped. With neck broken and air flow stayed, the giant deer slipped quietly into death. The cat still held his prey firmly. He breathed deeply through the corners of his mouth, and his chest heaved. The release of energy had been enormous, but he had killed as only a cat can kill, and he had killed well: a giant cat taking giant prey. Few animals on earth could equal the deed.

It was a full half hour after the wapiti died before the cougar began to eat. First he rasped his prey bare in several places, using the thousand hooks of his tongue, and then he opened the flesh there. He ate the heart, the liver, and other offal, then some muscle meat off a single haunch. He ate the sexual organs of the wapiti, too, and licked whatever blood seeped from the lesions left by his claws and teeth. He savored his kill, gorged himself, before covering what was left by dragging branches across the carcass and scraping pine needles onto the heap. He moved away, scratched up a small pile of earth and needles, and voided. He moved on a little farther, 25 feet from where he had dropped on his prey, and lay up in a tangle of roots from a wind-felled tree. He was distended and exhausted, and he slept easily. In twelve hours he would feed again. He would stay with the carcass for several days.

The cougar was programmed to defend his kill against any animal he could see who might wish to share his mountain of carrion flesh. But there were those he could not see. Beneath the seeping wapiti carcass, contact was made with the cryptosphere. Here, in the top few inches of forest floor, lived springtails, wood lice, centipedes, insects, mollusks, a vast assemblage of cryptozoa that thrive amid fallen leaves and needles, in humus, mosses, pebbles, fungi, lichens, and soil. Many of them feed upon carrion, as well as upon each other, and now a blanket of these creatures started doing from below what the cougar, their benefactor in this kill, had been doing from above. The bacteria were there, too, of course, converting chemicals, and as the disintegrating flesh seeped liquids down, the amoebas hunted up from their sea of soil liquids. Thus an entire cryptic world came together on the spot, and although the individual claims made by each creature might be small, their total was enormous.

All creatures on earth can be traced back to aquatic ancestors, and so dampness remains for most a critical matter. Desiccation is the foe of the cryptozoa of the forest floor, and a great wapiti dead and decaying beneath a pile of rubble is a sea of liquid nourishment seeping down through the soil. No sooner had the wapiti died than his distribution had begun. The microscopic ones would continue their feasting even when the cat returned hours later, and for days thereafter until only the final remnants of bone and dentine were left. Eventually the bones would be pulled apart and scattered, and much of their material used, leaving only the teeth, for they are the hardest parts of all. They alone could last longer than even the forest itself. They are usually the last record of such struggles. Three forms of life—the mighty cat, the second greatest of all the deer in the world, and the least of the cryptic animals—huddled in the soup and mash of decay.

The eagle stirred, for she was hungry again. She stared off into the dusk and spotted a new kind of movement and heard a new kind of sound, one beyond the hiss of the wind. A wolf pack had come along the ridge. The wolves had taken a bighorn mountain sheep three days earlier, but now they hunted again. There were three adults—an alpha male and his mate and a younger male—and four leggy cubs. The cubs were boisterous, and the adults were having trouble herding them through the mist that roiled around them and marked their movements, pocked by each footfall, swirled by each nervous lash of tail.

As the small pack emerged from the lower edge of the fog, they were no more than 100 yards from the upper limit of the conifer stand. The large male wolf gave a short, sharp signal, a kind of snarl that, while not yet aggressive, was clearly assertive and meant to be obeyed. The cubs stopped their tumbling play and cowered near their mother. She moved over to an out-cropping of rock, and the cubs followed. Minutes later the large male and his mate entered the forest 50 feet apart, heads down, tails down, the fur along their spines semierect. The younger male was stationed halfway between the rocks where the cubs hunkered down at the forest's edge. The cubs themselves were silent. All this had been organized by a single com-mand from the alpha wolf and by millions of years of species success.

The wolves found no suitable prey. They did find where a fox had long since covered the remnants of a feathered kill, and although the female carried a wad of bones and feathers around for several minutes while the others quartered the grove, there was nothing there really to sustain them. They found the skull of another fox, and although the male pawed it and whined, there was nothing there either. They missed the more recent wapiti kill by a little more than 100 yards. Ten minutes after they had entered the wood they emerged again, but it was too late. The young male wolf was facing up the slope, snarling, savage with rage. Three cubs instead of four hugged in against the face of the rock that rose from the slope like a small monolith. Just beyond it the golden eagle stood her ground in her shrouded fighting stance. Her wings were spread wide, their primary tips dipping to the ground as she covered her kill. Her mouth was open, and she hissed her warning, flames in her eyes. Her talons were closed on a small female wolf cub, whose hind legs were still twitching and whose eyes were only then riming over with the ice of death. The talons had closed through the rib cage and pierced both lungs. Red froth and drool spelled the mortal wounds.

The reaction of the wolf pair was immediate. They exploded up the slope. The eagle tried to lift away with the cub, but she was too heavy for the bird. As she beat down the slope to become airborne just over the wolves' heads, she dropped the cub. The wolves would mourn her before they left. Later the eagle would drop to earth again and feed on what could not be returned to life. She would then return to her tree. It was not time yet for her to quit the valley, its woods and its slopes. She would know. She would be called away when it was time. The beckoning signal would be internal, and it would tell her to seek a mate, other food, or another place.

15

The lion lay up in the area for six days. Several times during that period he circled the grove, deposited his scats, and then returned to his kill. He would lie on the decaying carcass, eat some, roll on pieces he pulled loose, and then close his eyes and sniff at the excavations his jaws had left. He would snarl menacingly when any smaller creature made noises in the surrounding brush or under the leaves. The hosts that fed on the carcass from the underside were hidden from him as they continued the conversion and distribution of wapiti substance night and day, humming as they munched their share of the vanishing deer. If amplified, the noise would have sounded like a sea pounding on a harsh and resisting coast. Massed on the underside of the carcass, this life

147

was itself a churning universe. Eggs were laid, and other creatures fed on these eggs as well as on wapiti.

And then the cat had had enough. The meat, what little was left intact, was very high and soft. It squirmed with boring insects and other converters that had moved up inside it. Far into death, it now seemed to have gained a new life of its own.

After one last perfunctory feeding, the puma spent about ten minutes covering what was left. He had no particular reason for this dead-end bit of behavior, but somehow it seemed important to the cat to cover what was left, and under the great tree, not far from the eagle, he scraped leaves and branches over the shards of wapiti on the forest floor. It was a feline ritual, a farewell to the scraps of another life that had meant life to him.

The male puma walked away and didn't look back. He came to the edge of the evergreen forest and stopped. With the benign look that cats assume at such times, he stretched his hind legs and voided. He stared up the slope, up to where the ice fields marked altitude and the preview of seasons. He stared and then scraped a small amount of dirt over his mark. Again without looking back, he began ascending the slope. He passed through one more area where trees grew and then emerged onto an alpine meadow. He was above the trees now, high enough above the ocean so that no tree could grow, and still he ascended. There was interesting lesser game in this higher region for hunters with speed and agility. Among the rocks there would be pikas, small-eared relatives of the rabbits and hares.

Although they would be hard to catch, they would pro·
vide a game. Whistling to one another across the echo-
ing hills, they would warn of the approach of the great
cat, just as they would of an eagle. They moved on
open, bare rocks, on which they spread their grain to
dry. Because their world was high and open and
brightly lit, they were diurnal creatures, even more
conscious of a predator's approach than animals on
lower slopes in darker places. Sheep came here, too,
but now there were only rock-hard, pellet-sized scats.
The puma found no promising sign of a live sheep
hunt.

In time the cat came to a place where water took on
new forms. Water exists in every living creature; none
can do without its internal share for so much as a second. That is true of the mountain lion no less than it is
of man, jellyfish, or amoeba. It is the substance of all
being, but only in that narrow temperature band when
it is a liquid.

The water that fell on the mountain was not as pure
as might be thought. On their way down, rain, sleet,
and even snow collect carbon dioxide, chlorides, sul-
fates, nitrates, and ammonia, along with organic and
inorganic dust. Snow is the cleanest precipitate of all,
but other rains are rich and brothlike with impurities.
As temperatures vary, water can be a solid, a gas, or a
liquid, even stages in between.

It was late in the afternoon when the cat arrived on
the high slope, and still the slanting rays of the sun
were warming. The water that rested in small seas in
the dense tundra underfoot was still liquid. But it was

growing colder as the angle of the sun's rays flattened, and by the time they paralleled the slope, radiating up instead of down, the change had begun in the water there.

Dew from that morning, puddles of previous rains, washes from snow that had melted in the small ovens where rocks met and formed dents—all these began to change. What had been liquid when the cat first arrived moved into an intermediary stage. It was an almost undetectable gel, at the gateway between liquid and solid. Still the temperature dropped. A thin crust formed. By now the cat was silhouetted against a moon made large and red by the lens of the debris-laden sky, a lens composed of sands from as far away as North Africa and of the spewings of volcanoes in Italy and Hawaii. Ice was on the high land, and with every step the cat's feet crushed it and made it crinkle like cellophane. The air was thinner and colder, the world paler here high above where the wapiti had died. The cat, a seeker of diversity, had come here for a change.

He rested, and his breath vaporized in the high night air. Higher yet, far above the cat and the mountain itself, other water vapor floated and eddied. With the quick, continuing drop in temperature, it began to precipitate out and to crystallize as its weight increased. In time it was snowing in the sky. But the winds were strong, and little of this snow fell to earth. Only the faintest dusting told of what had occurred in the high atmosphere dented by but still above the mountains. The scattering that reached the cat and adhered to his fur was a form of snow known as diamond dust, crys-

It was snowing in the sky- it was more a silver wash than an inundation.

tals no more than 0.005 inches across. It was more a light silver wash than an inundation. It coated rocks, too, and blades of grass.

From the warmer and moister regions below, a fog began creeping up the mountain, first in tentative fingers, then in a roiling mass. As it encountered the colder air, it became rime, feathery, opaque ice some people call hoarfrost. The snow that was reaching the high slopes descended through a mass of water vapor and picked up a coating. Its tiny flakes lost the feathery whiteness we know in the valleys and assumed what the old-timers who moved across mountains called soft hail or at times graupel. The mountain had become a dream place, a real world made unreal, and the cat, save for one owl, was alone.

So through the coldest hours of the night, water in many forms painted the mountain and the cat, a certain prediction of the winter to come eight to ten weeks hence. In the morning the cat's new world thawed. The sun warmed the rocks and the grass and the fur of the visitor from below. He lay cross-pawed on a high ledge and looked out across cloud layers, thinking whatever thoughts occupy a cat whose gut is full. In time he stood, yawned, and stretched. Then he shook himself, raining crystals all around him, as a last reminder of the night's cold and water's changeability. His breath still vaporized, but this would last for only a few more minutes. His bulk was great in proportion to the exposed area of skin through which he could lose heat, so he had not been bothered by the cold.

The cat moved down the hill. He was becoming hungry again and would use a slope 3,000 feet below the peak to hunt ground squirrels and lesser rodents. He did well, for voles were plentiful and quite careless as they hastened into tunnels with their winter store of seeds and vegetable debris. The cat ended their lives with playful slaps. He could eat two dozen in a single day. He filled up on these tidbits and never thought of a main course.

Another cat had moved into the hemlock forest below, a cat lesser in size but not in spirit. The female bobcat, working up from below, had entered the forested area the day before the mountain lion made the wapiti kill. She and others of her kind moved through the area every month of the year, but now she had a mission. She was looking for more than voles; she sought a place to bear her cubs. Fifty days before, in a midnight caterwauling session that had shaken the mountain, she had mated with a rough young male. Two days later she spit at him and slapped at his head when he approached her again. He moved away and in five days had another mate. But now, inside the female, four cubs grew, and fifty days later she was within a week of giving birth. She needed privacy and sought it in a place she knew to have wind-felled and otherwise distressed trees. She found a great trunk lying half buried near the giant Douglas fir. It had become a nurse log, and four new trees had begun to sap its substance. Several dozen seeds had sent shoots over in an arch, and they, too, sought foundation in the log.

The tree had been dead before it fell, with rot set into

its center portion. Heartwood had been eaten away, and at one end there was a hollow. It was a small cave, but large enough to hold the bobcat's 23 pounds of bulk. She crawled inside and began clawing at the wood. It was soft and gave way easily. She excavated a deeper inner chamber and over the next few days carried grass and leaves and other debris inside. She never seemed to be satisfied. There was always more to do as the birth of her cubs came closer.

On her fifth day in the forest she gave birth, deep in the fallen log. Where ambitious young trees throttled the nurse with their roots, she easily produced four more of her kind. She was a solid cat, built broad and strong, and her cubs did not have to fight hard for their first air. With her eyes half closed, making barely audible sounds, she bore them one at a time, each head first, each full of life and ready to struggle even though its eyes were sealed and it was, in fact, quite helpless. She cleaned them, licked them free of birth liquids and the placenta that had shrouded them inside her, and in their new dark place they began to squirm. She settled them down to feed them. They were her first, but she contained all that she needed to know. Each thing was done in turn, each move expert in the end, if hesitant at the outset, as she waited for her inheritance to deliver instructions and skill.

The most precocious of the young cats would open its blue eyes in four days. The smallest of the litter would take ten days to accomplish the same thing. For those first days the small cats lived by taste and smell and touch. Their mother was the world, no less than when she had carried them inside her. The log had become a second womb.

The female would nurse her young for two and a half months and during that period of time would display courage and rage at the slightest sign of intrusion. The delivery of her cubs had immensely increased her already innate potential for ferocity.

Soon after her cubs' birth, ravenously hungry, the bobcat began making short forays out from the log. After first checking to be certain no danger was at hand, she moved in an arc to seek small rodents. She ate little before rushing back to her nest. Her cubs' safety was an obsession. She was troubled by it, as she would not be with subsequent litters.

On the fifth day after her short hunting sallies had begun, the bobcat was even more nervous than usual. Something bothered her, and although she stopped beside every tree and mounted every log, she could neither see nor hear any detail that could account for her unease. At one point she ran up the trunk of a tree to a height of 12 feet, moving vertically as easily as most animals move on a horizontal surface. From her perch she looked around. Her nest log was still in view, so she climbed higher. Still unable to find anything, she simply dropped from the tree and moved off, circling her log at a distance of never more than 30 feet. She was seeking small rodents, though more anxious than ever to get back.

She found a vole at last and was munching on it, her back momentarily to the nurse log, when a strange new noise caught her attention. A man could not have sensed it, but the cat knew instantly that trouble lay behind her. Above her the golden eagle moved uneasily and looked off farther across the slope. The great bird had come and gone many times since her first selection of the tree. She had taken to flying off in the daytime, for the prey base on the slope was good and sustained her, but always coming back at night. She was little troubled by the drama below, although she could see much of it.

Deep in the nest log, the largest and most precocious of the little cats, the first one to have opened its eyes, was becoming adventuresome. It tottered toward the lighted opening, seeking information about the world that signaled to it from beyond the ragged hole, the hole through which its mother moved every day. The young cat neither heard nor saw what was waiting beyond. Before it could react, a paw shot in and nails impaled it. With the faintest squeal it was drawn out through the opening to where waiting jaws ended its life.

The male mountain lion had returned from the icy slopes. He had come again to the forest and found the log where the four young cats huddled. It was a simple kill. A mountain lion has long front legs and incurving claws of great strength.

The female bobcat flew along the top of the log, scattering debris and needles behind her. She landed on the larger cat's flanks with a scream that brought every hearing creature in the grove to full attention. The response from the mountain lion was an equal explosion and a scream like that of metal on metal. It is a unique thing, the sound of a cat in pain and rage.

The fight was brief. The bobcat could not best the puma, and to die herself would mean her remaining cubs would die as well. She had driven the puma a dozen feet away from the end of the log, and that was enough. Inside, she drove the three other cubs ahead of her to the deepest place. Then, hunching to face the open end of the log, now safely distant, she allowed the cubs to nurse. She could see the puma in the opening, his great yellow face peering in. Her ears were back, and her eyes glowed in the dark, flashing hatred as her heart pounded and her muscles remained drawn like coiled steel.

The puma had been hurt, though, and set to licking his wounds. He had not been able to react in time, and the single slashing assault by the enraged female bob-cat had done its work. One of his flanks lay open for 18 inches, and there were several puncture wounds in the other. He ached, and he was angry, but after licking himself, he walked over to where the tender kitten had fallen. He sniffed it, then carried it off and ate it lei-surely. Its feline nature was not a factor. He needed protein, and that was what he had found and taken. He fell asleep with the kitten's head, all that remained of it, between his paws. The eyes were still blue.

For several days after that, usually early in the day, the mountain lion approached the log. Each time he could hear the bobcat humming her rage inside, and each time he moved away without choosing another fight. On his last day in the forest he tentatively pushed one paw inside and felt around. When he withdrew his leg, it was open to the tendons. He jumped away as the pain shot to his shoulder and chest. He moved on,

She had long since forgotten that there had once been four.

limping downhill from the forest, stopping often to lick his latest wound. A year would pass before his next return.

In three weeks the bobcat, too, would abandon the area near the western hemlock and the Douglas fir. She would move across a slope farther uphill, away from the route taken by the puma, and seek a softer winter in a deeper valley, her three cubs following at a safe distance. She had long since forgotten that there once had been four. It was all the same. Two lives had begotten what survived as three more, each growing ever more complete in the skills and power needed to survive further. The fourth cub had been a safety measure, an affordable surplus of feline kind.

16

Once again the cycle had turned, and it was time for the night to retire to the west. From the east, beyond the ridges and slipping down like hungry orange fingers into the valley, the day was reborn. The sun had come across the North American continent after crossing the Atlantic Ocean, as it had come to that ocean from Europe and Asia. It carried with its own constant cycle the thousand biological cycles of the plants and animals that depended on it.

To avoid competition they could not tolerate, the species within each system had sorted themselves out to match the movements of the sun across the face of the planet. There were the diurnal ones, animals like the tree and ground squirrels, which awoke at first sun and retired long before purple dusk shaded into black night. There were the nocturnal species, like most of the owls and the flying squirrels, which hunted and were hunted only at night. Some species like the bobcat and the mountain lion were more conditioned to man than to the sun. They hunted day or night depending on how close they were to human habitation. Many species were crepuscular: they chose the dawn and hours near dusk. During the heat of the day and in the dark of the night they would lie up and wait. Many of the deer were like that, and frequently the bears. Snakes chose early morning and late afternoon if the nights were cool and the days hot. The sun touched all species and intruded upon all internal clocks, with both its seasons and its daily distribution of light.

Two deer on the slope, below the snow line but farther up than the highest tree, even farther than the last and most stunted bush, faced into the sun and were set aglow by the fire of early daylight. Their antlers looked blurred, glimmering in orange, and when they moved across the ridge, moving in silhouette, it seemed as if they were floating on a sea of flames.

Birds moved everywhere—stirred, shook, twittered softly since they were not yet awake enough to state imperatives of territory and other claims, and shook their feathers again. Some fluttered down from night branches and started to peck among the debris, beginning their day of hunting that would end the lives of millions of lesser creatures. In the first alpine meadow upslope, small seed-eating birds swayed on fronds and stalks and reedlike stems, pulling small, nutty fruits loose and blurring like the deer antlers in the new sky.

Other creatures stirred everywhere, some in retreat from the light, some toward it, all in rhythm with the sun that had come so far in its single revolution around a spinning globe. The first streaks fell to earth on the forest floor, painting ferns and mushrooms and seedlings.

The golden eagle, from her perch on the western hemlock, saw much of the drama of the dawn unfold. Looking off into the valley, she saw little but sky and the spires of lower forests. When she looked up the slope, however, she could see the other players come onstage, this morning as on all the others.

She had watched the bear shuffle down the mountain and had seen the cougar come and go for nearly a week. The bobcat had slipped in unseen, using the understory for cover, but the eagle had soon known the cat was there.

The slope above was rich in rodents, the same prey that had attracted the cats and given the dainty fox hopping games to play in the deep grass. The eagle had fed off those slopes and sometimes in the valley beyond the ridge where the mountain lion spent its arctic nights, but every day for three weeks she had come back to her perch on the hemlock. At times, looking off to the sky, she had seen what to man would have been a mere speck, and even that uncertainly seen. To the golden eagle it was another of her own kind. In each instance she had called in her little mouse voice, watching the speck advance and recede, play with the thermals and be gone. Still, she had stayed on, for an eagle's game of life is not specks in a distant sky but small movements in the grass.

She released a stream of liquid dung that splattered on needles, branches, and cones. She had done that often over the past weeks, since she came to the forest, and the tree bore the unmistakable mark of a roosting place.

The day before had been warm, the warmest that month, and the ground and vegetation had absorbed much of the heat. Then during the night, cold air had moved across the ridge and spilled down the slope like a broad river. Well before the morning sun had followed the air spill, the slopes had begun to steam. The air close to the warm ground was saturated with moisture, but because it was warm, it was also buoyant and rose to mix with the cool rivers of air slipping by. Condensation was immediate. Two moist parcels of air, with different temperatures, created an oversaturated mixture, and the excess water formed a cloud only inches from the ground. Thermals rising through the steam twisted and spiraled, as if the mountain were breathing, and the breath condensing.

Every blade of grass the sun touched, every leaf and every twig glistened with water droplets that had condensed on the cooling surfaces during the early hours before dawn. Spider webs, too glorious for princes, sparkled, their every steel-hard strand strung with water jewels. The webs, in the forest and in the meadow, numbered in the millions.

Overhead, cumulus clouds were evaporating as rapidly as they formed, and oceans of airborne moisture were in turmoil. Higher, farther off toward a distant ridge, rising cumulus clouds had flattened out into anvils on contact with a shearing icy wind. The temperature had dropped below −40 degrees Celsius, and glaciation had occurred. The glaciated clouds were now breaking up and spreading out in mile-long ice fibers in the sky.

We can only speculate on the ring of incentives that surrounds each of the animals that comes into our view. For the eagle sitting on her now familiar perch there were negative incentives, and positive ones as well. Since the prey base provided by the slope was intact, there was incentive to stay. Since no other of her kind challenged her domination of the area around the forest, she, again, might have reason to linger on.

But what of seasons? What does a golden eagle seek as the year moves through its four quarters? In spring an eagle may seek a mate, but now it was fall. Eagles tolerate cold weather well and need not migrate up and down mountain ranges as hoofed animals do. If snow falls too heavily, an eagle can kick loose and in minutes make a journey that might take a landborne animal weeks to accomplish. Still, there are seasonal movements among all birds, and the exact nature of the incentives are not always clear. We do not know why some birds migrate while others of the same species do not.

The eagle on her perch was surrounded with incentives felt only by her. She was urged and tugged and perhaps jostled by the need to select, decide, and respond. The things that were happening inside her are mysteries to us. Our catalog of food, shelter, mate, play, and escape are not enough; there must be others.

The eagle shook herself, fluffed out her feathers so

she appeared momentarily to grow, and looked out as she had every day since choosing the western hemlock perch. She ruffled her feathers again, called to the sky, then lifted her tail. Hesitantly, because she was not yet sure of the morning currents, she spread her wings. Without effort she dropped off the branch, sailed low until she was skimming the grass on the slope by inches, and then lifted. She banked and turned upslope. Each feather was a wing, and each wing a machine of flight. She caught a rising current. As she passed over the ridge, she seemed to falter, rocking from side to side in the face of the wind, but then she righted herself and dropped out of sight, just over the crest. She was sailing down another slope and would lift again on another avenue of air. The forest dwellers could no longer hear her small voice. But another eagle did, and she answered.

No creature in the forest knew or cared where the golden eagle had gone. While she was there, she had played her role, had been a member of a community. She had killed what she needed, had produced energy, consumed it, converted it, and had left behind the slag from the furnace of her accelerated life. The community she left behind, like any community at peace with itself, where life and death are in balance, would do as well without her as it had with her services at hand. The glorious golden eagle had come and was now gone. The forest still stands, and someday there will be another hunter on a transient mission—to come, use the forest, be used by it, and either be consumed or pass on. Everything that comes to the forest adds to it and is

No creature in the forest knew or cared where the golden eagle had gone.

added to, made more whole, more complex because of the life that stirs there in one grand mix. The system works—it accepts, receives, and in the perfectly impersonal way of a five-billion-year-old planet tumbles forward toward unknowable goals. The forest, like each of its tenants, is in evolution. What it will be when a billion more eagles have come and gone we do not know. But we do know that it must survive to achieve its destiny. And as long as the forest survives, so will its guests, those that dwell there for all their lives and those that, like the eagle and our attention, come and go.

Afterword

As I hope has been apparent in this book, I have gone to the woods, and I have wandered there and wondered at what I have seen. I have never had the good fortune to see either the fisher or a mountain lion in the wild, but all the other species described in the foregoing pages I have observed firsthand and with respect.

In fact, I have been visiting forests of one kind or another since I was a small boy, starting in my native Massachusetts. There have been many here in America—in fact, in just about every state where woodlands are still to be found—and many in Africa and Asia. There have been forests in strange, remote places like New Zealand, Sri Lanka, and Bangladesh. Wherever I have gone, if there have been woodlands, I have somehow gravitated to them. The species of plants have varied enormously, and so has the animal life, but there is a sameness in all forested areas. That universal quality is a sense of completeness. A forest *is* a place. For any moment it is a total system, just like the one described in this book.

But no one can contemplate a forest today, the one in this book or any other, without a sense of foreboding or even dread. It has been calculated that the tropical rain forest is disappearing at the rate of 50 acres a minute, night and day, every day of the year. If the assault on all forests were to be calculated, it is quite possible that two or three times as many acres per minute may be falling—perhaps as many as 150 acres every sixty seconds.

Surely that is not progress. We do need forest products, but the harvest should be orderly, the yield calculated, and the replacement planned before the harvest begins. But we need not dwell on this horror. Having read this book, you should be numbed by the prospect of all free, wild forests vanishing within the next fifty years—and that could happen.

All forests? What about those in parks and preserves? The trees will remain standing, but the forests themselves will become progressively more barren. As I hope this book has shown, forests must have a give-and-take relationship with their surroundings. Life-forms come and go, move from one forested area to the next. If the only forests left a half century from now are bounded by fences, then these islands shall cease vectoring life to other areas and will not receive life in return. They will be too far apart, too bulldozed, too homogenized, too sanitized to exist in anything but symbolic form.

I shall continue to go to the forests and walk in them and listen and fill myself with their greatness and quiet. Fortunately, one does not have to go far. When I visit San Francisco, Muir Woods is only a few minutes' drive away, and there one can enter the cathedral where all deities surely dwell. When I am in New York City, the Hudson Valley and the New Jersey Pine Barrens are near at hand. Close to Miami are the hammocks of the Everglades, and throughout the Southeast are splendid woodlands full of enchantment. Near Tucson there is the great Sonoran desert with its massive saguaro cactus trees. How different these places are from each other, yet how much they have in common. No rule holds for one that does not hold as surely for all the others. In each there are reptiles and amphibians, mammals and birds, insects, arachnids, and lower forms of life. The relationship of one species to each of the others is unlike any other set of relationships but, at the same time, exactly the same in end effect. If you have walked quietly in one forest, you have walked in all the forests that have ever been. And you should care very much whether there will be any left intact, fulfilled and complete, a half century from now. The thought that there might not be I would rate a nightmare.

Roger Caras
East Hampton, New York

Fauna That Appear
in *The Forest*

173

Flora That Appear
in *The Forest*

About the Author

Roger Caras is the author of over forty books on nature, the environment, and companion animals. He is a special correspondent on those subjects for the ABC News Television Network, the only correspondent assigned full time to those topics by a network. He is also a commentator for CBS Radio on pets and wildlife and is a pet columnist for *Ladies' Home Journal*. Mr. Caras was a recent recipient of the Joseph Wood Krutch medal for "outstanding contributions to the betterment of our planet" and of the "Fido Award" as 1977's Dogdom's Man of the Year. He is an adjunct Professor of English at Southampton College; a Lecturer in Animal Biology at the School of Veterinary Medicine, University of Pennsylvania; and a Fellow of the Royal Society, London. He has been awarded a Doctor of Letters degree by Rio Grande College. Mr. Caras is married and has a son and a daughter.